CONTENTS

INTRODUCTION – KEY CONCEPTS AND THEORIES

You will not be directly tested on sociological concepts and theories in the AQA Sociology AS exam. Nevertheless the key concepts and theories in Sociology are like the border pieces of a jigsaw and, once they are assembled, it makes the rest of your sociological study easier to fit together. You can just go through this section quickly and refer back when you need to. My advice, however, would to spend a reasonable amount of time developing a sound basic knowledge of concepts and theory. This will make the rest of the course easier.

SOCIOLOGY – THE STUDY OF SOCIETY

Sociology is the study of society. More specifically it is the study of human behaviour, and the way our behaviour is affected by the groups we all belong to. Of course sociology is not alone in studying human behaviour, Psychology and the other social sciences all study different aspects of behaviour. What social sciences have in common, and what makes them different from other ways of studying behaviour is that they adopt a **systematic** or even **scientific** approach. The novelist, poet, even journalists all study behaviour, but for different reasons and in different ways.

A Definition: Sociology is the **systematic study of human behaviour**, of the way in which **people interact** and **how their behaviour is conditioned by their membership of different groups.**

Sociologists, unlike journalists or authors are trying to produce "true to life" **(valid)** accounts of social behaviour. To do this they use systematic methods like questionnaires and observation, to try produce unbiased **(value free)** accounts. Compare this with a journalist who may be selective and sensationalist in his approach – after all he/she is not necessarily after the complete truth if it is boring and does not sell newspapers!

Sociologists vary in their views of **whether sociology can really be scientific**. Some sociologists emphasise the importance of **'verstehen' – the ability to empathise with people** and see the world as they see it. So as well as being systematic we must try to develop empathy and a **'Sociological Imagination'.**

Some people see Sociology as "Common Sense" but in many ways it is the exact opposite. Common sense is a mixture of experience, what our friends and family think, information from the media and school etc. So it is a mixture of 'facts', prejudice, bias etc. and is often superficial. As sociologists we must not only ensure our findings are unbiased we need to '**dig beneath the surface'** to find out what is really going on – appearances can be deceptive.

Sociology is important in influencing **social policy** – the actions of the government and its agencies. For example in recent years education and crime policies have, as we will see, been greatly influenced by **New Right** sociologists.

Concepts, Theories and Perspectives

Concepts are simply "**key ideas**" in sociology. Sociology also attempts to develop **Theories** i.e. **explanations/statements about how the social world works**. These theories may be tested **empirically** i.e. by doing research and finding out the **facts**, which are then used to test the theories. In simple terms a sociologist (like other scientists) will come up with a **Hypothesis** (possible, unproved, explanation for something) and then **test** it through research. A "proved" hypothesis becomes a theory – though it is arguable that any hypothesis/theory can be totally proven.

Perspectives are different ways of looking at society. They are a combination of concepts and theories. Unfortunately in Sociology there are many different perspectives which take a different view as to how society works.

Sociologists believe there are **patterns** of social behaviour. This is because we are all influenced by the groups we belong to so, to a certain extent, we behave in predictable and similar ways. A simple example, in school students wear uniform, this is because they are encouraged/persuaded to do so by the school, their family etc. But of course we should also remember we are also all unique individuals who have choices, so we do not necessarily conform all the time. Society is made up of many different **institutions** – family, school, work, media etc which all connect together to form the **Social structure** of society. The term **Social system** is used to describe these institutions and the way in which they, and the individuals who form them, interact with each other.

Different sociological perspectives place a different emphasis on the importance of the individual in society. Some sociologists argue that wo/man is, through the socialisation process, very much the product of society and the groups she/he belongs to (a **Structuralist** approach) i.e. '**Society makes man**'. Others emphasise that it is wo/man that creates society through his/her everyday interaction. (An **Interpretive or Social Action** approach) '**Man makes society**'.

Some Key Concepts

Sociologists see human beings as **social creatures**. We prefer to live in groups (as do most higher mammals) and it is the influence of these groups that forms and shapes our behaviour. This does not mean that biology/genetics plays no part in our behaviour but, in the endless '**Nature versus Nurture**' debate most sociologists are firmly on the side of nurture.

Culture

Culture consists of the beliefs, behaviours, objects, and other characteristics common to the members of a particular group or society as a whole. Culture includes language, customs, values, norms, mores, rules, tools, technologies, products, organizations, and institutions (for example the family, education system, religion, work etc. Individuals and groups tend to define themselves according to the cultures they belong to. This however is not a simple process. There are many subcultures within complex societies that can have different and sometimes opposing norms and values to the dominant culture of mainstream society.

Social identity

Social identity is a person's sense of 'who they are'. Tajfel and Turner (1979)argued that a person's social identity is based on their group memberships. We all belong to a range of different social groups and these groups (e.g. social class, family, peer group, ethnic group, religion etc) are an important source of pride and self-esteem. Groups give us a sense of social identity: a sense of belonging to a like-minded community.

In order to increase our sense of self-worth we tend to emphasize, and often exaggerate, the qualities of the groups we belong to – 'Manchester United are the greatest football team in the world', 'England is the best country to live in'. The negative side of this, of course, is that other groups may be put down and discriminated against – 'Chelsea are rubbish', 'the Italians are cowards.' The groups we belong to are often called 'in-groups', those we don't 'out groups'. The prejudices we hold against other groups can sometimes be a cause of discrimination (against other ethnic groups or religions for example). In the most extreme forms they may result in violence and even war.

Socialisation

Is the learning process we go through that transforms us from a "human animal" into a "**social being**". We learn the **Culture** – way of life - of our society and, most importantly, the **Norms, Values** and **Roles** we need to fit in to society.

Rewards and Punishments (sanctions) are used to encourage "good" behaviour and discourage "bad" behaviour. There is enormous pressure on people to "fit in" and **conform.**

Exercise – Think of some examples of how rewards and punishments are used to make children conform.

Cooley defines two stages of socialisation :

Primary – the first stage where the family is responsible for teaching basic skills, norms, values etc.

Secondary – where other groups/institutions become important – peers, family, school, media etc . Socialisation is not a process that stops when we "grow up". It continues throughout life as we enter new relationships, jobs and other social situations. Nor should it be thought of as a negative, controlling force. Without socialisation human beings are totally inadequate and unable to operate in society as is shown by examples like the "wolf children" Amala and Kamala who were found in India. They exhibited no traits of human behaviour and were, in effect, 'human wolves".

Roles

Are the "parts we play" in society. We all play many roles everyday. We do not simply interact with each other as the unique individuals we think we are but through the particular roles we are playing at any one time – daughter, student, friend, shop assistant etc. The relationships we form whilst playing our roles are called **Role sets**. Sometimes roles may be difficult to carry out – e.g. being a parent to a difficult teenager! We call this **Role strain**. Sometimes we will have to carry out more than one role at a time, and these may clash. We call this **Role conflict**. A working mother for example may often experience role conflict. People also do not necessarily play the same role in the same way, for example you may have a strict father or a lenient father i.e. they have different **Role styles**.

Status

Status is the amount of **prestige** or social esteem attached to a particular role or position. **Occupation/job** is a major definer of status in our society where most status is **Achieved** i.e. the result of our own efforts, ability or talent. Status however can also be **Ascribed** i.e. based on inheritance (e.g. the Royal Family) or other characteristics (like ethnicity) you are born with and cannot change.

Values

The way we play our roles is strongly influenced by our **values.** These are **general guides to behaviour**, the things that we feel are important and worthwhile. In The Western World for example most people strongly value "money success", we also tend to think things like freedom, individualism and respect for life are very important. These general values are carried out through a vast number of norms.

Norms

In our everyday lives there are vast arrays of **norms** which guide our behaviour. **Norms** are s**ocially acceptable, expected ways of behaving** in different situations, and are strongly influenced by our values. **Laws, rules, mores and customs** are all types of norms. In the classroom, at home and at school we all carry out these norms e.g. in the classroom we go to our seats, take out our files and pens, face the teacher etc. We don't usually think about this, we do it automatically, according to the role we are playing.

Roles, in effect, consist of a whole range of norms.

Of course both **norms and values vary greatly from society**. In our society for example we greatly value money success and work hard to achieve it (norm). North American Indians valued generosity and it was the norm to give wealth away.

Power and Authority

Authority is the legitimate or socially approved use of power. It is the **legitimate** power which one person or a group holds over another. Power can involve coercion and involve the use of force or violence Authority, by contrast, depends on the acceptance by **subordinates** of the right of those above them to exercise power over them.[

Traditional Authority: Power legitimized by respect for the past and established customs and norms e.g. Kings, Tribal chiefs.

Charismatic Authority: Power legitimized by extraordinary personal qualities/abilities that inspire subordinates to devotion and obedience e.g. Religious figures like Jesus or Buddha, or great military leaders like Hitler or Genghis Khan.

Rational-Legal Authority: Also known as bureaucratic authority, is when power is legitimized by the law 'written rules and regulations' usually made by the State and is often based on the position/job a person holds.

Of course these types of authority don't just exist in their 'pure form' A schoolteacher may have traditional authority (because teachers have always had respect!?) , certainly bureaucratic authority, but also, if they are an inspiring teacher, charismatic authority.

Evaluation

So far we have presented these concepts as if they were not problematic but, as you will see; different theories see them in somewhat different ways. Many **"socio-biologists" argue that genetics have far more influence over our behaviour that sociologists allow.** Marxists and Feminists criticise the way that socialisation, in their view, is used to oppress the lower social classes and women. There is also the question as to what extent we simply "take up" the values etc. that are given to us and to what extent we may rebel. Furthermore to what extent is it really true that there are common values and norms in society?

These concepts will crop up in all the topics you study and it is a good idea to get a clear understanding of them early on in your course so that you can easily apply them later on. Issues of Culture and Identity and Power and Authority are central to the course, whether we are examining family roles, religious groups or how schools operate (and many more topics).

Test your understanding of Sociological concepts

1. Explain the difference between primary and secondary socialisation.
2. List the roles you play in your everyday lives.
3. Produce a brain map/diagram to show your "role set" either at school or work.
4. Using examples explain the difference between "role strain" and "role conflict".
5. Outline the values and norms in your friendship group – be clear about which are values and which norms.
6. Explain, with examples the difference between achieved and ascribed status.
7. Explain, with examples the difference between power and authority.
8. Explain the link between roles, values and norms.

Sociological Theory

Sociological theory is, of course, central to your understanding of sociology and should play a vital part in all your essays – indeed it is impossible to get the highest grades without theory. In the three main sections of this book different theoretical approaches to the family, education and methods are dealt with in some detail. This section provides a basic outline of general sociological theory, greater depth will follow.

Sociology was born in the **Enlightenment** – this was when the **modern world** as we know it began (around the 18th Century). Before this time religion dominated the way people thought about the world but in the modern age of cities and factories **science** became the key to explaining both the Natural World and society.

Auguste Comte is usually credited with being the first sociologist. He developed the ideas of **Positivism** – a scientific approach to the study of society that argues that sociology can be just like Natural Sciences such as physics and chemistry. This is because Comte believed there were **laws of human behaviour** just like the laws of gravity or natural selection. Human beings have to follow these laws or patterns of behaviour so **behaviour is predictable** and can be **measured in numbers**.

Karl Marx, Emile Durkheim and Max Weber – the 'Founding Fathers of Sociology' *(Adapted from Public Domain images)*

We can discover these laws through scientific study and learn to predict and control human behaviour. There was a great belief in **progress** at this time and scientists (including sociologists) believed that through scientific, rational study we could make a better world.

Structural functionalism
Founder: Emile Durkheim

Functionalism is a **Structuralist, systems** approach i.e. it looks at the whole of society and the way in which we are "**made**" to follow certain patterns of behaviour by the institutions/structures that produce and control us – family, school, media, religion etc.

The job of the sociologist is to discover and explain the **functions** (parts played) by the family, school etc. in ensuring a stable, healthy, society.

6

Functionalists compare society to a living creature (**the 'organic analogy'**). Just as all the organs of a living being (heart, brain, lungs etc) perform their own functions in keeping the body healthy, so the institutions of society play their roles in keeping society in a stable, ordered, condition. Like the organs of a body these institutions have to all work together and if one fails it can have a disastrous, even fatal ,effect.

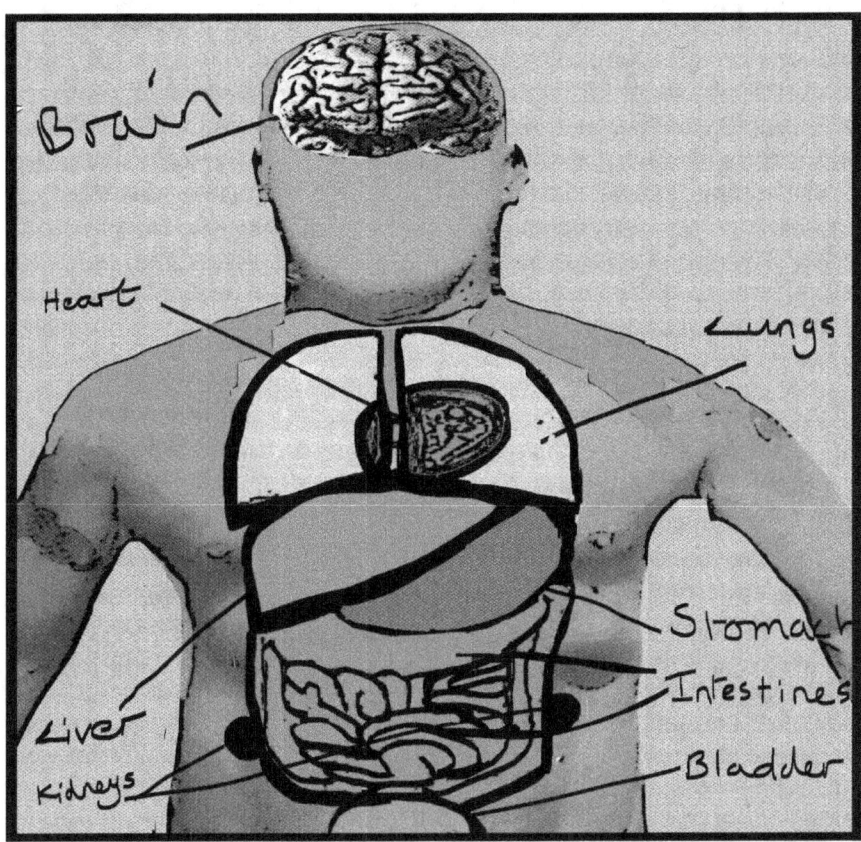

Functionalists argue that societies are, and must be, based on **value consensus** i.e. **shared basic values (norms and beliefs)**. This is what makes order and stability possible. If people all had different values etc they would be "pulling in different directions" and there would be strife and conflict everywhere, leading to societal breakdown. But the family, school etc socialise us into these common values etc. from birth.

The reason there is value consensus is that we are taught (**Socialised**) from birth into learning the **Culture** of society. The values, norms, roles etc, that society needs us to carry out. These become part of us (they are **internalised**)

Evaluation

Functionalists are criticised for being **deterministic**, according to them people have no choices or free will, they have to follow the patterns set down by society. They are also seen as **conservative** – supporting the system and justifying inequalities. Because they see order and stability as 'normal' they find change and conflict hard to explain. Also do people really have common values in our society with its many different social, ethnic and religious groups?

Test your understanding of Functionalism

1. What do Functionalists mean by value consensus? How do they think value consensus comes about?

2. Think of arguments/evidence/examples that support the view that there is value consensus in society and arguments/evidence/examples that go against this idea.

(Structural) Marxism

Founder – Karl Marx

Like functionalists Marxists take a **structural (systems)** approach to the study of society. They do not however see society as being based on consensus, but on **(class) conflict.**

Marx argued that society was formed by the relationships people enter into as they produce the material things they need in life – food clothing shelter etc. Those who control the M**eans of Production** (in **capitalism:** the technology, factories, banks etc) are able to **dominate** and **exploit** the people who work for them. These relationships between "bosses and workers" Marx calls the **Relations of Production.** Workers (**the proletariat**) are exploited by the owners (**bourgeoisie**) in the sense that they are paid less than the value of the work they produce, the owners take this surplus in the form of **profit.**

There is thus always a conflict of interest between the owners, who seek to maximise their profits, and workers, who strive to obtain the best possible wages and conditions – **class conflict.** Marx thought that when workers realised the true nature of their exploitation – became **class conscious** - they would overthrow capitalism and, in time, establish a new system based on the common (joint) ownership of the means of production – **communism.**

The rest of society – the **Superstructure** – is built on, and determined by the economic system. **Our legal, family, educational and all other social systems serve the needs of capitalism** and the **dominant class** (the bourgeoisie). In fact the whole **culture** of society is based on the economic system.

Like Functionalists Marxists believe that we are socialised to fit into society, but the values and norms we learn are those that suit the Capitalist system – **they are the values, norms, beliefs etc of the dominant class** – Marxists call this **Ideology.** Because those at the top control education, the media, religion etc (Marxists call this the **Ideological State Apparatus**) they are able to control what we learn and know.

Evaluation

Marxism, like functionalism can be criticised for being **deterministic -** some Marxists see people and their behaviour as the direct product of economic forces. **Weber** argues that the Marxist view of class is simplistic there are many different classes and social groups in society – ethnic groups, women etc. Like functionalists Marxists can be seen as **biased – against capitalism**. There has not been a revolution in capitalist countries and most w/c people are now better off. The so-calledCommunist societies were characterised by oppression and have failed.

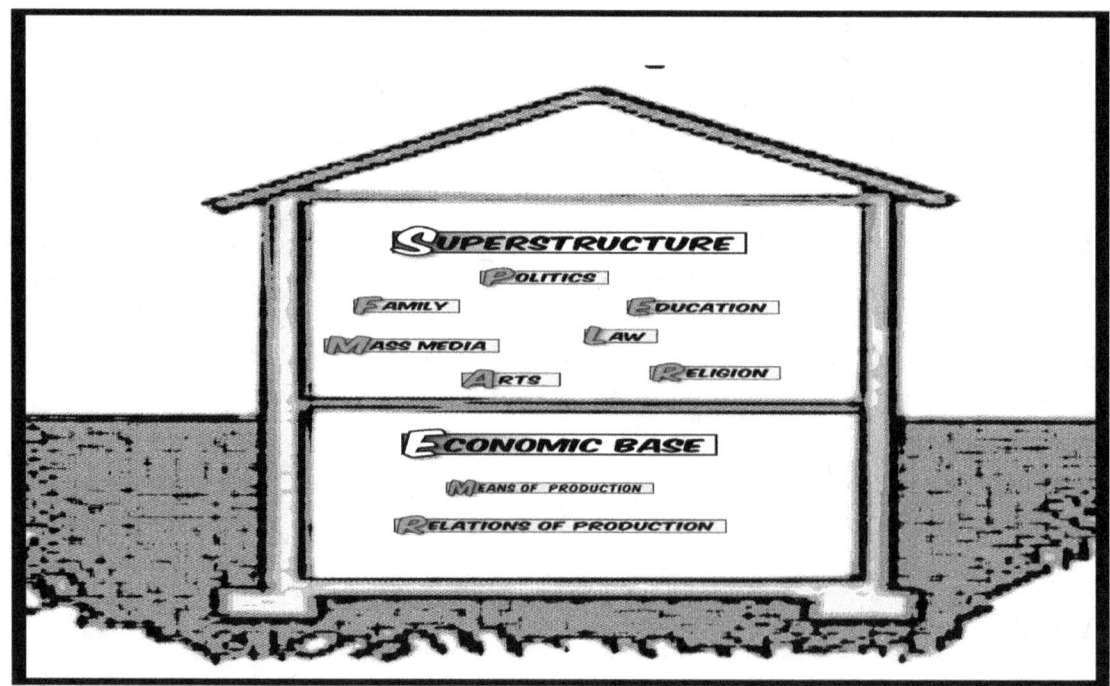

> **Test Your understanding of Marxism**
>
> 1. What is Ideology? What role does ideology play in maintaining the capitalist system?
>
> 2. Why do Marxists believe that society is characterised by class conflict?
>
> 3. Identify and explain two similarities between Functionalism and Marxism.
>
> 4. Identify and explain 2 differences between Functionalism and Marxism.

Social action approaches

Founder – Max Weber

Weber, like Marx and the functionalists, believed in a "scientific" approach to the study of society. However he was also the first to develop what is called **social action theory** arguing that **people are not merely the product of structures in society but active participants who have choices in how they act.** The way people behave is determined by how they define social situations – the **meanings** they attach to them. in order to understand behaviour you have to **empathise (verstehen)** with people- see the world from their point of view.

These ideas have been developed into **Interpretivism or Interactionism. Interactionists** argue that wo/man is the creator of society through his/her everyday interactions with other people – **wo/man makes society** and we have choices in how we behave.

Interactionists emphasise the importance of **symbols and sign**s, especially language, in making sense of the world. It is the **meanings** we give to situations that determine our actions. We all look for clues – signs and symbols - in order to decide how to act. One of the most important concepts that Interactionists use is **labelling.** This describes the way we put people or groups into categories, often **stereotyping** them. Sometimes people react by living up to the label they are given, we call this a **self-fulfilling prophecy.**

Exercise – To understand this better think of the ways in which Teachers may label pupils. What effect might this have on pupils? Are you labelled?

Evaluation – Interactionists are criticised for underestimating the control that society and its institutions have over us. Because they concentrate on the individual they can't really explain how societies work.

> **Test your understanding of Social Action theories**
>
> 1. Explain in your own words the main differences between structuralist and social action approaches.
>
> 2. Why do Interpretive sociologists emphasise the importance of verstehen/empathy in sociological research?

Feminism

Feminist ideas can be traced a long way back in history. Many of the earliest civilisations worshipped an "Earth Mother" goddess and women had high status in such societies. In the early part of the 20th century, in Britain, the "suffragettes" played a big part in the emancipation of women. It is however with the French philosopher **Simone De Beauvoir** that modern feminism really began. De Beauvoir was a Marxist and used Marxist ideas to demonstrate that women, under capitalism, were an exploited group. The term **"Sex class"** is some times used to show how women are used as a reserve army of labour under capitalism and as carers for male workers and children (the future workforce of capitalism).

There are several different forms of Feminism – **Liberal/Reformist, Marxist/Socialist and Radical** (more on this later), but all agree that societies are characterised by **Patriarchy** – male dominance.Feminists accuse sociology of historically focussing on the concerns and behaviour of men of being patriarchal or **'malestream'**. They examine the ways in which institutions like the family and education maintain patriarchy and serve the interests of men.

Evaluation

Feminists have been criticised for being "anti-men" and anti-family – again taking a biased approach. They are accused of damaging the family and being responsible for beliefs that have increased divorce and breakdown. Feminism is also very splintered. **black feminists** accuse Feminism of being white and middle class.

Test your understanding of Feminism

1. What is **patriarchy?** Can you think of any examples of patriarchy e.g. in the family, media or at school?

2. Why do Feminists criticise **malestream** sociology?

The New Right or "Neo-cons"

Since the 1970s the "**New Right**" has been very influential in Sociology and society in general. Sociologists like **Charles Murray** are very 'pro-capitalism' arguing that it is not only the most efficient economic system but also guarantees freedom and human rights.

The New Right are associated with socio-biological approaches seeing inequalities as genetic. W/c and blacks do less well at school and work because they are less able!

The New Right are highly critical of left wing and liberal attitudes towards things like crime, welfare and education. They argue that the Welfare State has produced a benefit dependent "**underclass**" who are prone to crime and have a something for nothing attitude. Benefit cuts, more prisons etc. are needed to deal with problems in society.

The New Right believe that 'market principles' should be applied to most, if not all, areas of social life. Schools, doctors and hospitals etc. should compete for clients and funding should be based on how successful they are – those that fail to attract enough customers should be shut down. This, they argue will improve standards and give the consumer more choice.

Evaluation

The New Right are criticised for blaming the poor and underprivileged for their own problems for justifying the system and its inequalities, and ignoring the impact of class, ethnic and other inequalities on educational achievement and family life.

Test your understanding of the New Right

1. Why are the New Right so supportive of capitalism?

2. How do they explain inequalities?

Pluralism and the Postmodernist challenge to Sociology

Pluralism accepts that there must be a degree of value consensus in society but argues that societies have become much more diverse in recent years – **we now live in a pluralist, multi-cultural society with many different ethnic, religious and other groups.** Power is spread throughout society and Marxists are wrong to argue that society is controlled by the "Ruling Class".

Postmodernists reject 'grand theories' like Functionalism and Marxism arguing that they are just 'meta-narratives' (big stories!) and that all explanations of society have similar value. **Lyotard** argues that in contemporary postmodernist societies the effects of social factors like class, ethnicity and gender are lessened. Our identities are no longer determined by our background but "chosen". This has been made possible by mass production and the mass media which offer a vast choice of goods, services and ideas from which we select to form our identities.

Evaluation

Postmodernists have been criticised for **relativism** and superficiality. They argue that any view is as valid as any other. Critics argue that through logic and evidence we can establish which theories are better. Also progress and science have bought great benefits to people – medicine, food, living standards etc. Postmodernists also underestimate the choices people have – only the relatively well off have much choice of identity and factors like gender and ethnicity still have a huge effect.

10

Test your understanding of Postmodernism
1. In what ways do Pluralists criticise the Marxist view of power?
2. How do Postmodernists say that identity and culture are formed in contemporary society?

Public Domain Image
Postmodernists argue that today's pluralist, multi-ethnic, society is characterised by a diversity of norms and values.

AS/ALEVEL SOCIOLOGY TOPIC 1: THE FAMILY
THE FAMILY INTRODUCTION

The family is the most basic of human social groups in society. All societies have some form of family structure. Almost all people experience living in a family for at least some periods of their lives. Because of this we tend to "take the family for granted" and do not think about the essential roles it plays in society and in **socialisation.** For most people the family is the institution that provides the first, vital stages of socialisation, teaching us the basic skills, values, norms and roles we will need to become an effective member of society.

Family and households

Learning objectives

Knowledge and understanding of the definitions of the family and household.

Knowledge and understanding of the nature of different types of family.

Family and households are not the same thing. A **household** is simply a group of people who live together, so they may not necessarily be related e.g. a group of students or friends who live together or, increasingly, people who live alone – unmarried, divorced, widowed etc. In the 2001 census there were over 26 million households in the UK, most contain families but an increasing number do not. All families are households but not all households are families.

A family is a type of household where people are related by blood, marriage and/or adoption. These are usually **kinship groups** where people are related by blood or marriage – parents, children, grandparent, cousins etc. but may also contain foster children, adopted children, step children etc.

The Nuclear family is the basic family, consisting of two generations – parents and dependent children living together. During the 20th century there was a big increase in the number of **independent nuclear families** as economic changes required families to be more economically and socially mobile (to move for jobs or better housing etc.)**The Extended family** includes 3 or more generations of the same family living together or close by with frequent contact and some **interdependence** (i.e. they rely on each other socially and/or economically). These became less common in the 20th century because extended families are less mobile (see above). Nevertheless most families maintain contact with their wider kin – via the telephone, visits and e-mail etc. They also 'help each other out'. **Finch and Mason (1993)** found that 90% of their sample had received or given financial help from their extended family.

In recent years moreover many grandparents are increasingly looking after their grandchildren because both the children's parents go out to work. Moreover as family size decreases relationships between grandparent and grandchildren become stronger (and longer lasting as life expectancy for the elderly increases). Children thus often maintain regular contact with grandparents, and families where this is the case are often called **beanpole families**- because they are 'long and thin' with fewer wider relatives like aunts and uncles, but may 'stretch' to four generations. According to the **Office of National Statistics (2004)** 61% of grandparents see their grandchildren at least once a week and 78% at least once a month.

Test your understanding.
1. What is the difference between a family and a household?
2. What is the basic difference between nuclear and extended families?
3. Is it true to say that nuclear families are now, mostly, independent of wider family?
4. Why are 'beanpole families' so named?

Many Grandparents are playing an increasing role in taking care of their grandchildren whilst mum and dad are at work.

FAMILY DIVERSITY IN MODERN BRITAIN

Learning objectives

1. Knowledge and understanding of the range of family forms found in Britain today

2. Analysis and evaluation of the reasons for increasing diversity.

3. Analysis and evaluation of theories of family diversity.

4. An awareness and understanding of examples of the diversity of family forms in other societies.

The classic study of growing family diversity in Britain was conducted by **Robert and Rhona Rappaport (1982 and 1989).** They argued that the nuclear family was no longer the dominant type and that the growth in diversity was a positive thing reflecting freedom and choice, and the growing equality of women. Feminists also tend to welcome the decline of the traditional, patriarchal, nuclear family which, they argue, largely benefits men, though the **New Right** are highly critical of these developments **(see theory below).**

The family 'life-cycle'

Before we accept the view that the nuclear family is rapidly declining we should consider the **family 'life-cycle'.** In modern Britain it is highly likely that most people will experience a variety of family forms in their lifetime. Let's take an example. We will call her 'Brittany'. Brittany is born into a **nuclear family** but at the age of ten her parents split up and divorce, so she now becomes part of a **single-parent family**. At the age of thirteen however her mother sets up home with her 'boyfriend'.

Brittany now lives in a **cohabiting family**. A year later her mum marries her partner and he brings two of his children, from a previous relationship, to live in the new household. Brittany is now part of a **reconstituted family**. At the age of 18 Brittany goes to University and shares a house with friends (**a communal household**). When she leaves University she gets a job and rents her own flat living in a **singleton household**. She starts to date John, and after six months they move in together (**cohabiting couple**). A year later they marry and within five years have had two children (**nuclear family again).** The children move out and Brittany and John are left alone (**empty nest family**). At the age of 75 John dies and Brittany is left to live alone again, **as a singleton.**

This pattern of family, and variations on it, are not uncommon. Note also that for long periods of her life Brittany is part of a Nuclear family. This is the point that **Robert Chester** makes in **The Neo-conventional family (1985).** He argues that family diversity has been exaggerated. Most cohabiting couples marry and become nuclear families. Most single parent families come from

13

nuclear families and many marry again. In addition most singletons eventually marry or, in the case of the widowed, have already been married. In short the vast majority of us spend a great deal of our lives living in nuclear families. For Chester the really significant change in the family has been the increase in wives who go to work. This is what makes the Neo (new) conventional family. The government regularly produces a set of **official statistics** called **Social Trends**. This contains data from the **Census** and other research and is invaluable to sociologists in giving up to date, **Quantitative** data that shows changes and developments in Britain.

Methods link - Official Statistics such as these are vital when looking at nationwide trends. No sociologist would have the **time or money** to conduct huge surveys like the Census (which is sent to every household in the country and has to be completed by law – another thing we sociologists are unable to insist on!) Such surveys have **huge samples** and are likely to be **representative and reliable**. They do, however have the limitations of all surveys – **lacking the ability to get the meanings and reasons** behind people's responses and, of course, people may misunderstand questions, lie or give socially desirable answers, therefore their **validity** is questioned.

In terms of the family what these statistics show is a great increase in **family diversity** since the middle of the 20th Century. It is very difficult today to talk about 'the typical British Family' in the 21st Century. The **"cereal packet family"** of two parents and kids is still common but by no means predominant.

The family and household in Britain today – the facts:

The following types of families/households are increasing – single-parent families reconstituted / step-families, cohabiting couples (many with children), singletons and same sex families.

There are now over 26 million households in Britain – up by over 35% since 1971.

The average number of people per household has declined. The number of households with 5 or more people has fallen from 14% to 7%.

This is not because of an increase in Nuclear Families - the percentage of households containing families with children has fallen from 52% in 1961 to 36% in 2010.

Probably the biggest changes are the increase in single person households (up from 11% to 28%) and lone parent households (up to over 2 million lone parents in 2011)

There has also been a big increase in **reconstituted families** (those containing step children/parents), this is largely the result of increased divorce. About 8% of households contain reconstituted families.

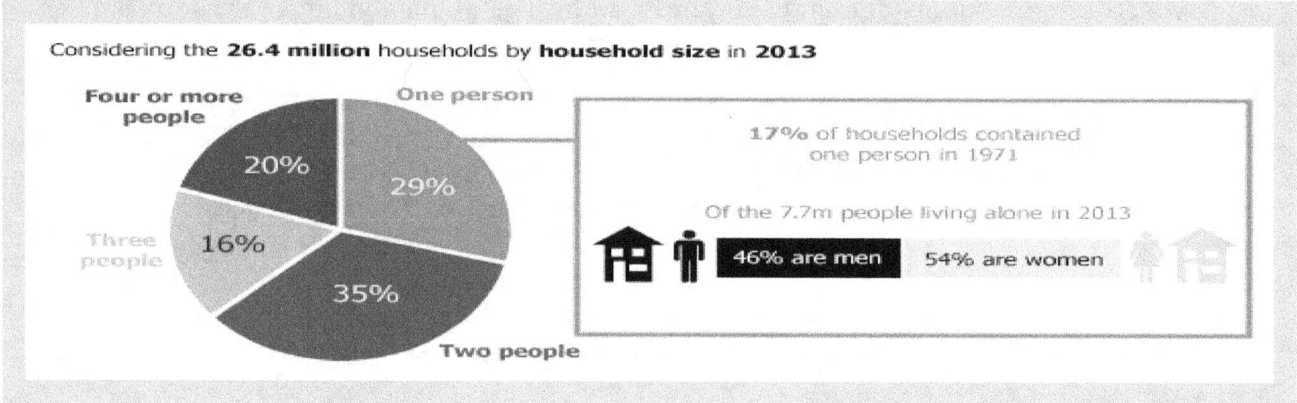

Considering the **26.4 million** households by **household size** in 2013

Four or more people 20%
One person 29%
Three people 16%
Two people 35%

17% of households contained one person in 1971

Of the 7.7m people living alone in 2013
46% are men   54% are women

Source O.N.S.

There is little doubt therefore that the family has become more **diverse** i.e. there are a far more different "types" of family. We should however bear the following points in mind. **It always pays not to take 'facts' at face value:**

14

1. The figures for the number of nuclear families seem low, but the figures are given as percentages of households – most households contain couples, single people etc. so the actual number of people living in Nuclear families is much higher. For example about **78% of children in Britain today do live in some kind of Nuclear family** (if one includes lone parent families etc.)

2. We should also remember that people (especially women) live much longer today. Elderly widows make up a lot of single person households and this is one of the reasons for the increase in such households.

FACTORS CONTRIBUTING TO INCREASED DIVERSITY

Social Class

Middle class families are more likely to be Nuclear. This is because the divorce rate is much lower than for working class people and middle class girls are far less likely to become 'unmarried mums'. Working class areas, particularly in inner cities, may still have elements of the extended family,and they also have far more single parent families. **Charles Murray (a New Right theorist)** argues that this is because of the development of an **underclass,** 'below the working class' who are often **dependent on benefits** – unmarried mums can get benefits and housing and so are encouraged to become single mums. (**See New Right theory below**).

There are other differences between m/c and w/c families:

M/c families are more likely to employ au pairs or nannies to look after their children when they go to work, whilst w/c parents are more likely to rely on family or friends.

Children from upper and upper m/c families who attend public schools as boarders live away from home for long periods of their childhood.

Some research indicates that w/c families are more likely to physically punish their children than m/c parents.

W/c marriages are more likely to end in divorce – this is, at least partly, associated with higher levels of poverty and the stresses this produces. An old w/c saying "When poverty comes through the door, love flies out the window".

Sexuality

In the past gay and lesbian families were not included in the statistics (until 1978). Thus the number of such families was hidden. Now it is included, and growing. There are a number of reasons for this development:

The law has been changed, The Civil Partnership Act (2005) gave legal recognition to gay relationships. Changes to the adoption laws/guidelines (2008) also means that gay couples can adopt children. The legalisation of same-sex marriage also came into effect in 2014.

Increased social acceptance of homosexuality and 'gay families' (though the New Right and other socially conservative groups still condemn them). It is worth remembering that homosexuality was illegal until 1967. Now even politicians and celebrities feel that it is okay to 'come out'.

Secularisation/religious decline. Most religions condemn homosexuality as immoral but religion has less effect on social attitudes today. Indeed even religions have changed. There is an ongoing debate in the Church of England about attitudes towards homosexuality and 'gay priests'.

Technological/medical changes mean that Lesbian couples can use IVF treatment to get pregnant.

Research into gay and lesbian families is fairly new. **Weeks et al (1999)** found that many gay and lesbian families strive for relationships where there is more emphasis on equality and negotiation. The major criticism of such families is that children are likely to be damaged by having gay or

15

lesbian parents. Research, however, does not generally support this. **Fitzgerald (1999)** argues that there is little evidence of differences between the children of heterosexual and homosexual couples. What matters is not the sexual orientation of parents but the parent/child relationship. **Stacey and Biblarz (2010)** in their review of studies carried out in the USA found no difference between children raised by heterosexual and lesbian couples 'children brought up by lesbian couples are growing up to be just as well-adjusted and successful as children with a male and female parent'. (Note that there has been little research on the children of gay men because it is a such a recent development).

Ethnicity

We must be careful not to talk about ethnic minorities as if they were all the same. There are a variety of types of ethnic minority families.

Afro-Caribbean households are most likely to consist of single parent families – around 50%. These tend to be **Matriarchal (female dominated)** and are a continuation from life in the West Indies where unemployment and poverty meant that women were frequently better of living without male partners. They tended to rely on extended kin and other women in the same position. In Britain, where West Indian males also suffer from educational failure and high rates of unemployment, divorce rates amongst Afro-Caribbeans are high (as they are for whites – Asians tend to have lower divorce rates). **Mohood's (1997)** study of **Asian families** (these include Indian, Bangladeshi, Pakistani as well as Chinese etc.) shows much higher numbers of extended families. This partly reflects the culture of their original countries where extended families are the norm. It is also partly due to immigrants tending to move into areas of Britain where there are already ethnic communities and where they already have family ties. This gives them added support and security (sometimes in the face of racism). Low divorce rates are also part of their culture, and partly reflect greater levels of family control and religious belief. The practice of arranged marriage (and in a few cases forced marriage) remains. In many cultures the idea of marriage based on "romantic love" is considered strange. Marriage is seen as a joining together of families and as an economic and social union. Therefore it is essential that parents are involved in 'finding a suitable match'.

Some Asian families are changing. There is evidence that many **Indian families,** for example, are becoming more nuclear as they become more affluent and move into m/c areas. However wider kin tend to remain important and family gatherings include extended kin – birthdays, religious feasts, marriages etc.

Asian Extended Family Public Domain Image

Another change in recent years has been the increase in 'mixed' or 'multicultural' marriages and families. Elisabeth Beck-Grensham (2002) found that such marriages often face prejudice from their immediate families, because of their different ethnicities/cultures. In a few, very extreme,

16

cases this has led to so-called honour killings. However there are also optimistic signs; such marriages may help to break down ethnic boundaries and it shows that people are making their own choices, rather than obeying the cultural norms of their ethnic group.

Singletons

Singletons are people who live alone in a household. The number of singletons has increased (as we mentioned above). There are again several reasons for this:

The average age at which people get married/cohabit has increased. This means that many people in their twenties and thirties often live alone whilst pursuing their careers.

More men over the age of thirty live alone because of **increased divorce** (it is, in the vast majority of cases, women who get custody of children).

Women, on average, live longer than men, and life expectancy has increased. Therefore there are many widows living alone.

Reconstituted Families

Reconstituted (**or step or blended families**) are when two people, with at least one child from a previous relationship, marry or cohabit. This family form has grown significantly over the past 30 years as the divorce rate has increased, and now comprises about 10% of all families. The vast majority of such families, as one might expect, have children from the mothers previous marriage – 86% compared with 14% from the male partners, or both, previous families. Some studies indicate that children from reconstituted families may suffer numerous problems ranging from friction with step-parents to an increased chance of educational failure and a tendency to leave home at an earlier age. This is partly the result of a lack of clarity about boundaries and roles. Who is included in the new family? What rights has the step-parent (usually the father) in terms of disciplining the other partners child? Problems are often made more difficult if a child retains a strong attachment to the 'birth parent' who no longer lives with them **(Allan and Crow 2001)**. This may also be the reason why reconstituted families have high divorce rates (almost 50%).

Single-parent families

Perhaps the most significant change in the family over the past 40 years has been the dramatic increase in the number of single-parent families. Around 25% of all families in Britain today are single parent and 90% of these are headed by women. The percentage of single parent families in Britain, since the 1970s, has tripled and is the highest in Europe. Moreover, whereas in the past most single parent families were the result of the death of a partner, now most are the result of divorce or unmarried women having children.

Reasons for the increase in single parent families

The most important reason is the **increase in divorce.** In 1970 divorce became both easier to obtain, and cheaper. Divorce rates immediately rose to much higher levels.

Changing attitudes. Being a single-parent was once considered a source of shame, now there is far less stigma attached. The decline in traditional religious influence **(secularisation)** is part of the explanation for this, as is changing attitudes influenced by **Feminist** ideas. Other institutions such as the **media, education and the Government** have also adopted a more positive view towards single parent families. In general there has been a change in social attitudes towards greater tolerance of different ways of living and an acceptance that people have the right to choose their own lifestyles and family arrangements. There has also been a significant change in attitudes to marriage. Because of increased divorce and growing 'feminist' attitudes that women should be more independent, some women have elected to become mothers without husbands.

The growth of the Welfare State has enabled single parents to survive more easily by providing a range of benefits. Women no longer have to rely on a man to provide for them. Feminists welcome this development as it allows women to be more independent and to extricate

17

themselves from abusive relationships. New Right sociologists, such as **Charles Murray,** are critical of this, arguing that many single families are welfare dependent and young unmarried women are encouraged to have children by the welfare support they are given. They would point to the fact that 40% of single-parent families are headed by never married women (though the number of 'teenage mums' is less than one would think from reading the papers – about 5%).

The vast majority of single-parent families are headed by women (90%). There are several reasons for this, most revolving around the traditional belief that women are 'naturally' more caring and nurturing. When divorce cases come to Court judges tend to assume that women should get custody of children for this reason. The socialisation of women into caring, nurturing values means they are more likely to want custody of children. Men are more likely to be in well-paid jobs which they are reluctant to give up, and to see single-parent fatherhood as 'unnatural'. They too have been socialised into the view that women are natural carers. Men are also more likely to abandon their family, whereas women who leave their husbands tend to take their children with them – especially when women are seeking refuge from abusive husbands.

However recent years have seen the development of organisations like 'Fathers for Justice' who argue that the present system of custody is both discriminatory and unfair. They argue that men's rights, in terms of access to and custody of, children are being ignored by a system that favors women.

Criticisms of Single-Parent families:

Both **Functionalists** and the **New Right** are critical of single parent families arguing that one parent cannot effectively socialise a child. In particular the absence of a male role model may lead to lack of discipline and deviant behaviour – especially amongst boys. Research by **Mclanahan and Booth (1991) i**ndicates that children from single-parent families are less likely to succeed in education and are more likely to be delinquent. They are also more likely to become single parents themselves and to be unemployed and/or be in low paid jobs in later life. However we must be careful not to turn this correlation into a simple cause. It may be that the material deprivation suffered by single-parent families is a more important factor in explaining these differences.

Single-parent families are also far more likely to be **benefit dependent**. **Murray** argues that the 'something for nothing' values of such families are passed on to children who are also likely to become benefit dependent and resort to crime.

Evaluation

Many children from single parent families do well in education and achieve good jobs. Therefore it cannot just be the nature of single-parent families that causes problems. It is more likely to be the poverty that many such families experience (**Allan and Crow 2001).** Research indicates that when single parent families are financially better off and have the support of other relatives these problems are far less serious.

Also we cannot tell how such children would have 'turned out' if they had stayed in families characterised by conflict and abuse. **Cashmore** argues that 'one good parent is better than two bad ones'. **Feminists** support this point. Many single-parent families are the result of women leaving violent or abusive husbands.

Chester(1985) also makes an important point when he argues that being a single parent is often just one part of the family life cycle. Most single-parent families come from nuclear families and become nuclear again, when they find a new partner.

Modernity, late modernity, family diversity and the Sociology of Personal Life

Choice has become the 'buzzword' in 21st century society. Choice in education, choice in healthcare and choice in personal relationships. **Giddens (1992)** argues that we now live in a '**late modern' society** in which people have greater freedom and choice in all aspects of their lives.

People can choose their (family) relationships to suit their personal needs and identities. Marriage is based on '**confluent love**' deep intimate emotion, characterised by partners reve**aling their needs and desires to each other. Relationships only last as long as people think that these needs ar**e being satisfied

The old restraints of wider family, legal restrictions and economic dependence no longer apply. This view is taken even further by postmodernists who see society as being in a constant state of change and uncertainty.

These profound changes in the family have caused many sociologists to question whether we should approach the study of the family in the traditional way (with a focus on family structures and, in particular the Nuclear family). Instead they argue that relationships are so diverse **we need to examine relationships in terms of 'intimacy' and how relationships are negotiated** between ,for example, partners, parents and children, friends etc. Lynne Jameson (1998), for example, argues that 'intimacy' has come to replace what we have traditionally called 'primary relationships' showing a change in focus from the structure of relationships to their quality.

Sociologists such as **Giddens and Ulrick and Elizabeth Beck** argue that the traditional structures that underpinned heterosexual relationships (e.g. man - breadwinner, woman - housewife and mother) have been undermined by factors like increased divorce, women joining the labour market and the increase in women's independence. Giddens argues that this means men and women are much more able to create and organise their own pure relationships (i.e. based on love rather than traditional roles and norms) through daily actions and decision making. **Beck and Beck** produce a similar argument in terms of how love, sexuality and family life have changed and that intimacy is the basis for these new, individualised relationships – 'people are now free to write their own lifescripts'. The norms and structures that once constrained our behaviour no longer apply. **Judith Stacey (1996**), in a study in California found that there was no one family form or lifestyle that people aspired to, no generally agreed values and norms of family life. Stacey also argues that gay and lesbian families are an ideal model of postmodern kinship because they are free from the constraints of traditional patterns of family life and so can consciously develop their own intimate relationships. Studies have also shown that such relationships tend to be far more equal and democratic.

Some sociologists have a far more negative view of such developments, arguing that increased individualisation leads to selfishness and a lack of shared values which has produced a 'demoralisation of western culture' (**Fevre 2000**) leaving us confused, unhappy and insecure (one might apply **Durkheims** concept of Anomie here).

Other critics, including some Marxists and Feminists have argued that the ideas of individualisation and choice are grossly exaggerated. There are structural pressures on people from their families, culture and general economic and social conditions. Class and gender inequalities have enormous effects on peoples relationships – women, as we shall see, still do the vast majority of housework and 'caring' . Indeed it could be argued that women's position has, if anything, worsened with the growth of the **'triple shift/burden'**. The far higher rates of divorce amongst the w/c also indicate the effect of material deprivation on relationships.

Another criticism is that 'Personal Relationship theory' underestimates the diversity there has always been in family and kinship relationships, both historically (for example 'single mums' were a feature of the Industrial Revolution in Britain) and in terms of different cultures.

In addition arranged marriages as a form of social and economic contract still dominate much of the world and most people, even in our society, would probably deny that they freely chose to become a single-parent or get divorced.

A world of Diversity

When we come to look at the wider world the complexity and diversity of human forms becomes even more apparent. Indeed some sociologists suggest that in the face of such diversity the concept of 'family' becomes almost meaningless. Let us examine two examples: Marriage and family in the Trobriand Islands and amongst the Nuer of Sudan.

The Trobriand Islanders of New Guinea, live in a Matrilineal society – in other words inheritance, family name etc are traced through the mother. Indeed the Trobrianders believe that men have only a limited role in producing children. The spirit or Ka of the mother is what gives the unborn child its form and nature. The relationship between brothers and sisters is strong because it is a man's sisters children who inherit his wealth. Women move to their husbands village when they marry but send their sons back to their home village when they become teenagers to be cared for by their maternal husband.

The Nuer of Sudan, in contrast are a Patrilineal society, descent and inheritance come from the husbands family. A man will pay bridewealth for his wife, in the form of cattle. The wife then becomes a member of the husbands kin group. She works and produces children for this group. Even if the husband dies all her future labour and children still belong to this kinship group. She may be married to her late husbands brother or left unmarried to take lovers, but any children she has by her lovers will still belong to he late husbands kinship group!

Test your understanding

1) Explain the importance of the 'life-cycle' in understanding family diversity.

2) Why does Robert Chester believe that the 'neo-conventional' nuclear family is still the norm?

3) Explain the reasons for the increase in:

a) Same-sex families

b) Single-parent families

c) Reconstituted families.

4) Examine the ways in which migration to Britain has increased family diversity.

5) Why are the New Right so critical of the single-parent family?

6) What criticisms does Personal Relationship Theory make of traditional Sociological approaches to the study of the family?

Theories of the family- the roles and nature of the family

Learning objectives
1. Knowledge and understanding of sociological theories of the roles and nature of the family.
2. Analysis, comparison and evaluation of different theories of the family.

Functionalism

Until the 1970s the **Functionalist perspective** dominated the sociology of the family. Functionalists see every institution in society as being essential in ensuring the smooth running of society and in maintaining order through Value Consensus.

George Murdock (a functionalist) argued that **the nuclear family was essential, inevitable and universal**. In other words it exists everywhere because society (and people!) cannot do without it.

In his **famous study of over 350 societies (1949)** he found all had nuclear families. These were essential to perform **4 vital functions**:

Sexual – The family provides stable sexual relationships for adults and controls the sexual behaviour of its members.

Reproductive – produces children, new members of society.

Economic– provides for the material needs of its members – food clothing shelter etc.

Socialisation/Education – teaches the essential skills, norms values, roles etc. so that children become effective members of society, learning to "fit in" and obey the norms and rules – thus order and stability are maintained.

Murdock's definition of the family

'The family is a social group characterized by common residence (i.e. they live together), economic co-operation and reproduction. It includes adults of both sexes, at least two of whom maintain a socially approved sexual relationship, and one or more children, own or adopted, of the sexually cohabiting adults'.

In the 1950s another famous functionalist –Talcott Parsons - argued that the family, in Western Societies like the USA and Europe had become more **specialised.** The modern nuclear family has two basic/essential functions:

1. Primary Socialisation – teaching children to accept (and practise) the essential norms, values etc. needed for order and stability. Families are 'factories' producing new citizens.

2. Stabilisation of adult personalities. The family provides emotional support and stability for both parents and children (**affective function**) it is a source of stability and security helping us cope with the stresses and strains of wider society.

Functionalism tends to take a very positive view of the (nuclear) family and is open to many criticisms:

1. Murdock's definition of the family is criticised for ignoring the diversity of family forms – ignoring gay, single parents and other family forms.

2. Functionalism ignores the "**dark side of the family**" – child abuse, domestic violence etc. **Morgan (1975)** points out that there is no mention of alternatives to the family or problems in family relationships.

3. Marxists criticise functionalists for ignoring the way in which the family benefits capitalism, producing workers and socialising children into the ideology of the ruling class (see below - Marxism)

4. Feminists argue that functionalists ignore the **patriarchal** nature of the family – the way women are oppressed into a domestic role – housework and looking after children (and their husbands). The family makes women dependent on men. (**see below - Feminism**)

Key point - don't forget to use other theories to criticize functionalism!

The Nuclear family – a declining institution? Public Domain Image

The influence of Functionalist theory has declined since the 1970s, largely as a result of increasing diversity and conflict in the family and society in general. However it should be noted that these changes could be interpreted as supporting the Functionalist view. One could argue that it is the breakdown of the nuclear family that has increased deviance, crime and delinquency in society – the family is no longer performing its key functions – stabilization of adult personalities and socialization - as effectively. This is certainly the position taken by the **New Right.**

The New Right

The New Right has supplanted Functionalism as the most influential, conservative, perspective on the family. The New Right shares many of the views of functionalist sociology. It too argues that the traditional nuclear family is the basis for a stable and ordered society.

New Right sociologists such as **Charles Murray (1989 onwards)** relate changes in the family to wider social changes. Arguing that **the Welfare State has undermined the family** and that an **'underclass'** has developed. Members of the underclass have very different values and norms to the rest of society. They are prepared to live on benefits (and in some cases crimes - benefit fraud. petty theft etc.) and are not prepared to work. In other words thy have a **'culture of dependency'.**

Benefits have encouraged unmarried (often teenage) mothers – The rate of 'teenage pregnancy' is **nine times as high for young females from lower w/c backgrounds than those from professional m/c families.** In single-parent families the mother often does not work and children are thus brought up living on benefits and with **no male role model**. Easier divorce and the increase in reconstituted families have also helped produce what the New Right regards as a **'breakdown'** in traditional family values. Lack of discipline and respect for authority have lead to increased crime and deviance by young people – many families are **failing in their socialization function.**

> **Dennis and Erdos in 'Families without fathers' (2000)** sum up many of these ideas. They argue that children born outside marriage are disadvantaged in terms of health and educational achievement. It is particularly boys who are badly affected. They grow up without a male role model in the home, and do not develop the view that adulthood involves taking on responsibility for a wife and children. Many are thus socially immature, irresponsible and anti-social.

> **There are many criticisms of the 'New Right approach:**
> The New Right are criticised for focusing on the poor and blaming them for society's problems – 'blaming the victims'. Most so-called 'underclass' families are honest and work hard to provide for their children; often in very difficult conditions. So is this so called culture of dependency true?
>
> Poverty, and the stresses it causes, are one of the main causes of divorce and family breakdown. The New Right are quick to criticise but fail to identify the real causes of family problems.
>
> Feminists accuse the New Right of sexism, because of their argument that women should follow traditional roles as housewives and mothers.

Critical views of the family

Marxist theory and the family

Like Functionalists Marxists see the family as performing vital functions for society but they do not see this as a positive thing. Marx himself wrote comparatively little about the family but his comrade **Friedrich Engels in 'The Origin of the Family, Private Property and the State'** applied Marxist theory to the family, arguing that the family is part of the superstructure of society and its forms and functions are determined by the economic system. The family acts as a way of controlling women's sexuality and ensuring that men can pass their possessions on to their (male) children. The family is thus a source of both class and gender exploitation. In particular Engels, and the Marxists who followed him, examine the ways in which the family serves the needs of capitalism and the interests of the Dominant/Ruling class. **Marxists. argue that the family performs the following roles in capitalist society:**

The family provides an **economic function – inheritance**. The upper class (Bourgeoisie) pass their wealth on to their children, thus maintaining the privileged and dominant position of their children.

The family acts as a source of relief to (male) workers frustrations. W/C men may be alienated and exploited in their job but they are bosses in the home – this helps them accept their position in the workplace – and is thus functional for capitalism **(Zaretsky 1976).**

W/c women are also exploited. They provide care for husbands and children as housewives and mothers. This helps to produce a healthy and productive workforce for capitalism.

The family/household is a unit of consumption. The modern Nuclear family is isolated and easy to persuade to buy the goods – TVs, fridges, cars, DVDs, etc. that Capitalism has to sell in order to be profitable. The Bourgeoisie of course get the profits. The development of the mass media and advertising have increased this 'consumerism'.

Althusser sees the family, like education, as part of the **Ideological State Apparatus** – putting across the ideology – ideas and interests of the Bourgeoisie, through the socialisation process. It is therefore one of the agencies that supports the capitalist system.

Marxist analysis too faces many criticisms:

Marxists focus on the economic role of the family, and its benefits to the Bourgeoisie. It ignores the many positive benefits – love, protection, security etc. that the family gives to people and society.

The idea of women as a housewife/mother is outdated. Most women now work and are sometimes an equal or even the main wage-earner.

The family flourishes in all societies not just Capitalist ones. Even so called communist societies like China and Cuba have not got rid of the family. In fact in communal systems like the Kibbutz in Israel, the family has made a comeback!

Note - Both Functionalists and Marxists see the family as playing a vital role in reproducing the social structure of society – through socialisation, and thus providing control and order. The big difference is that Functionalists see this as positive, whereas Marxists as negative, as maintaining the inequalities and exploitation of Capitalism.

Radical Psychiatrists

In the 1960s a branch of psychiatry emerged that was highly critical of the nuclear family. **Leach(1967) and Laing (1964)** argued that the nuclear family acts like a 'pressure cooker'. The decline of the extended family means that parents and children spend too much time together, and there is no wider family to provide emotional support and an outlet when the pressure builds up. Parents pressure children and have too high expectations, children feel suffocated. Thus members of the nuclear family often take their anger and frustration out on each other, in the form of physical or emotional abuse, and these problems also lead to mental illnesses like depression.

Cooper (1972) focuses on children in the family and adopts a more Marxist approach, arguing that relations in the family resemble those in the workplace. Parents encourage children to be obedient, a quality they will need to have at school and work. They also pressure children into having 'realistic and respectable' ambitions in terms of jobs – and stamp on their fantasies and dreams.

These views are, to a great extent, supported by **Margaret Meade**, an anthropologist, who studied the lives of young people in Samoa. She concluded that young people in Samoa were far more happy and well balanced than those in Western societies because they had far less control and pressure from their parents and had a far less inhibited attitude towards sex/relationships.

> **Criticisms of these approaches:**
>
> **Laing and Leach** are too negative. They underestimate the continuing links between extended and nuclear family, and Laing exaggerates the relationship between the nuclear family and mental illness.
>
> **Cooper** also dwells too much on the negative aspect of parent/child relationships. Functionalists argue that the child-centered nature of the nuclear family means that children receive far more love and attention than they ever did.
>
> **Meade** has also been criticized for 'taking as true' the stories that children and adolescents in Samoa told her. Subsequent research suggests that they may well have exaggerated their freedom from control – and also their sexual activities!

Feminism

Feminists argue that society is **patriarchal** i.e. male dominated. Feminists tend to be critical of the family. Like Marxists and Functionalists Feminists see the family as maintaining the existing social order. They focus on how this affects women and, in particular contributes to the inequalities they face.

Feminists examine the way in which the family (along with the school, media etc.) reproduce patriarchy in society. The family from an early age teaches children (traditional) roles through the socialization process. Boys are supposed to be "tough, assertive, active" girls "gentle, passive, conformist" This is reinforced by the way they are dressed, the toys they are given and, in general, the way they are treated. Women are thus socialised to be dependent on men and to put themselves in "second place", their husbands and children come first. There is an **Ideology of Patriarchy** which is passed on through the socialization process, in the family and carried on into wider society.

There are 3 main types of Feminists, all of whom see the causes of gender inequality somewhat differently:

Liberal/Reformist Feminists emphasize the traditional cultural values and norms which are reinforced by the family. Through education and changes in the law women can achieve equality.

Marxist/Socialist Feminists see the roots of gender inequality in the Capitalist System. The family produces and cares for the current and future workforce. Women play a central role in this as housewife and mother – a role they perform for nothing as housework is unpaid. They are also a **reserve army of labour** – often part time and low paid. They are thus doubly exploited by Capitalism. In addition men often take out their frustration at work on their wives, often in the form of domestic violence. Women thus act as a safety valve for the capitalist system **(Ansley 1972)** who argue that women are in all ways 'takers of shit'.

Radical Feminists argue it is not just about capitalism Women have always been exploited. They argue that the root cause of this is the fact that women bear and take care of children. They are thus, for long periods of their lives, dependent on men. **Purdy (1997)** argues that motherhood is an expensive and long term commitment in terms of time and energy, She advocates a "baby strike" – only then would men take women's demands for equality seriously. Men will always oppress women because they are in a more powerful position. In the family it is men who get most of the benefit – women who do most of the work. Some Radical Feminists argue that women should separate themselves from men, and advocate "Instrumental Lesbianism" i.e. women should only have relationships with other women. All relationships with men are about domination and exploitation

Black feminism is critical of other feminists arguing that they are 'white and middle-class' and have tended to ignore the particular difficulties of women from different ethnic minorities – for example West Indian women who have to survive as heads of single-parent families and some Asian women who may suffer from even stronger patriarchal control than other women, and be subject to arranged or even forced marriages.

24

Criticisms of Feminist Theories

Feminists, like Marxists are criticised for taking a negative view of the family. Are there no happy families and marriages? Indeed the New Right criticises Feminists for undermining the family and blames them for much of the family breakdown of recent years.

Feminism has been criticised for being 'anti-men' and for undermining the role of fathers in the family.

Do men always dominate the family? Some sociologists argue that many husbands and wives share roles and power, particularly as more women work. However research by **Jan Pahl** shows that when both men and women work full time it is still women who do most of the housework and childcare.

Feminism is also criticised for assuming that women are passive and can't change their position, indeed for ignoring the many improvements women have made.

Many critics argue that, like Marxism and Functionalism, Feminists underestimate the diversity of family forms, and the choice people have.

Interpretive and postmodernist theory

Although these approaches are not identical they share certain views:
Both argue that the family today is characterized by much more diversity than in the past. There is much more **choice** about how we live because of social and cultural changes – there are nuclear, extended, single parent, step families etc. People may move from one type to another in different periods of their life. **Stacey (1990)** argues that western family arrangements are dynamic and fluid. No longer can one family type dominate. (See also 'Sociology of Personal Life' - above)
Postmodernists approve of this because people have more choice about their family options and can choose on the basis of their individual needs and lifestyle. We are no longer controlled by tradition. A good example of this is divorce. In the past people were forced to stay together by a combination of laws and social pressure (divorce was considered morally wrong). Now people no longer have to stay in "empty-shell marriages".

Criticisms

Critics such as **O'Brien and Jones (1996)** argue that this diversity is overstated, most people only live in one or two types of family during their lives, most spend a considerable amount of their lives in nuclear families.

Post-modernists are also criticised about their idea of choice. Do most people really want to get divorced or become a single family? There are other pressures on people and families today. The idea of greater choice and freedom is thus misleading. As usual it is the powerful who get the most choice.

Test your knowledge and understanding
1. Why do functionalists believe that the nuclear family is the ideal family form?
2. In what ways does Parsons think that the nuclear family has changed its functions? What reasons does he give for these changes?
3. Why are the New Right so critical of recent changes in the family?
4. According to Marxists what role does the family play in maintaining capitalist society?
5. What criticisms do Radical Psychiatrists make of the nuclear family.
6. How do different types of feminists differ in their analysis of the family?
7. What do Postmodernists mean by families of choice?

Demographic change and the family

Learning objectives

1. Knowledge and understanding of the nature of, and reasons for, demographic changes in the UK, including Birth Rate, Fertility Rate, Mortality Rates, Life Expectancy and Migration.

2. Analysis and evaluation of the effects of demographic changes on the family.

Demography refers to the study of population and changes in the population. These changes relate very closely to changes in the family e.g. as we have already seen migration into Britain has increased family diversity. According to the 1901 census the average married couple had a total of nine children, of whom three died in childhood. Average life expectancy was just over 40 years (though this was partly because so many children died at an early age). The population of Britain was just over 36 million. Britain today is a very different country in terms of its demography. Let us examine the changes that have occurred and the reasons for these changes.

Population growth. The population of Britain has grown to around 70 million people during the past century. This has largely been due to a reduction in death rates and a significant increase in life expectancy. At the same time birth and fertility rates have declined, meaning that families in the 21st Century are, on average much smaller. This development, along with increased life expectancy, means that Britain has an 'aging population' with far more people over the age of 65.

Changes in Fertility/Birth rate. **Birth rate** refers to the amount of children born to an average 1000 of the population per year. The Birth rate in Britain has fallen from 28.6 in 1901 to 12.2 in 2014.

The **Total Fertility Rate** is the measure that demographers usually use in their research. This refers to the average number of children a woman would have in her lifetime. In 1901 this was around 3.5, now it is around 1.93 (note this seems to contradict the figures for family size in 1901, but at this time many women were unmarried or died in childbirth so the average was far lower.

Reasons for the decline in TFT/Birth Rate

Decline in the Infant Mortality Rate – the number of babies who die before the age of one (per year, out of every 1000 born). This means that women do not have to have a large number of children as 'insurance' in case some die.

Child centered family – fewer children means better care, in material and emotional terms, for the children a family does have. This also means that the **cost of children has increased.** Research by insurance companies **like LV (2006)** indicates that the cost of raising a child and putting them through university has risen to £180,000. In another survey 20% of respondents said they would remain childless because of the cost and another 20% said they would have no more children, for the same reason.

Changing attitudes – **Sue Sharpe** interviewed girls in London in the 1970s and 1990s. She found that their priorities had radically changed and that the '90s' girls focussed far more on careers rather than family and marriage.

New opportunities - Girls are doing far better in education and there has been a **feminisation of the jobs market** (less traditional manual jobs and more white collar and professional jobs, suitable for women).

Individualisation and risk – Postmodernists argue that society is, today, characterized by increased choice. The old constraining norms like 'it is the role of a woman to marry and have children' have broken down. Women seek their own identities. This may, or may not, include marriage and children. The increased breakdown of marriage and families has led to greater uncertainty about commitment – relationships are seen as 'risky' and uncertain – children are expensive and may be disruptive to partner relationships and (women's) careers.

Women are having children at a later age – thus less time to have more children

Effective contraception – the 'pill' etc have given women greater control over their fertility.

Whilst the trend in fertility over the past 100 years has been downwards there has been an increase in the rate in recent years. **In 2011 fertility reached its highest level for 40 years**. In particular the number of women over 35 having babies more than doubled since 2001. Part of the reason for this is the increased effectiveness of IVF enabling couples/women who once could not have children to do so but it also reflects the general trend of women postponing having children until a later age.

Mortality Rates.

Death Rate refers to the number of people who die, per 1000 of the population, in any given year. The other key mortality rate in the **Infant Mortality Rate** (see above). **Life Expectancy** refers to the average number of years that a person, born in a given year, can expect to live. Mortality rates in Britain have fallen, significantly, over the past 100 years, (the Death rate from 18.4 in 1901 to 9.3 2014; the IMR from 142 in 1901 to 4.4 in 2011). Life expectancy has thus increased dramatically (women's life expectancy in 1901 was 49 years, now it is 82.8 years – for men the figure has risen to 79 years).

Reasons for the decline in mortality rates

One of the main reasons for the reductions in mortality rates in the early 1900s was improved public health. Clean water supplies and effective sewage systems dramatically reduced diseases like cholera and typhoid etc.

The introduction of nutritious school meals, along with school medical services in the 1900s reduced child mortality.

As did improvements in diet and housing standards. Absolute poverty was markedly reduced in the 20th century increasing peoples resistance to disease.

Medical improvements were also important – vaccines against diseases like Diphtheria, polio and TB reduced death rates – especially amongst children.

The Welfare State provides health, social and economic support for the vulnerable. Old Age Pensions have helped improve living standards for the elderly.

We should however note that there are big differences between the mortality rates of different social groups. Most of the differences can be linked to inequalities of wealth and income in Britain and have risen considerably in the last 30 years. The **London Health Observatory found the gap in life expectancy gap between people who lived in the most affluent and most deprived London areas was 25 years.** In general poor, w/c areas have far lower life expectancy – the North of England, Scotland (especially Glasgow) etc. This can be explained in many ways – poorer diet, housing, medical services, insecurity, smoking and drinking etc

Migration – refers to movement of people. **Immigration** is movement into a country. **Emigration** is movement out of a country. Britain is a society that has, throughout history seen waves of immigration – Romans, Angles, Saxons, Normans etc. In more recent times, around world war two a number of Jewish (and other) refugees came from Europe to escape persecution. The 1950s and 60s saw the encouragement of migrants from the old 'British Empire', mostly Asians and West Indians. These were recruited to overcome shortages in (mostly low paid) public services such as transport – but also health. To a certain extent this pattern of immigration has continued, though now there are now much tighter restrictions on migrants from outside the EU. The most recent wave of economic migration was the result of the expansion of the EU. Many Eastern Europeans have migrated to Britain in search of higher paid jobs than they could attain in their own countries, and have been eagerly welcomed by employers because they are ready to accept low wages compared to the indigenous population.

Immigration effects

Britain has become an increasingly 'multicultural society e.g. there are over a million people of Indian origin and a similar number of black West Indians and Africans in Britain today.

This has added to family diversity (see above).

Critics (New Right etc) argue that immigration threatens national identity and consensus, because migrants bring in different norms and values. For example West Indian families are often single parent and this produces delinquent (male) children, some Asian groups have a tradition of arranged or even forced marriage.

This leads to the thorny question of integration – to what extent should migrants adopt the culture of the country they now live in?

The recent influx of Eastern European workers (up to two million – estimates vary) has also produced controversy and problems. The fact that most of these young workers are singletons has increased pressures on housing and, where families have moved to Britain, there are increased pressures on education and social services. This is partly due to the fact that migrants are often concentrated in specific areas, where their may be work available, or where family and friends already live. By 2014 the Net Migration rate (the ratio of people coming into the country minus the number leaving) was 2.56 migrants per thousand of population.

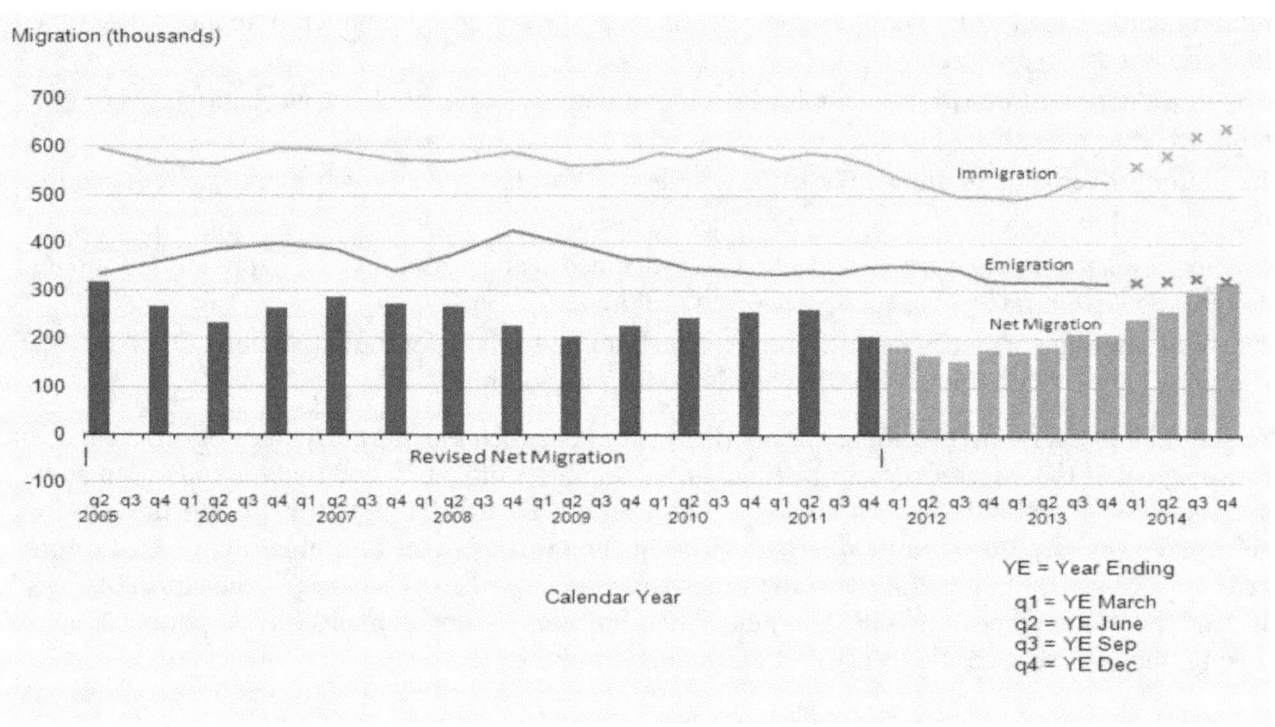

Source ONS

Emigration from the UK has also increased over the last decade. The number of Britons leaving the country has gone up by a third since the mid 1990s. Since the year 2000 over one million UK citizens have left the country (though there has also been an inflow of 600,000 UK citizens). The reasons for emigration are many – work, retiring to the sunnier climes of Spain or France, the hope for a better living or lifestyle in countries like Australia.

In general migration is on the increase all over the world as improved transport enables more people to move around and the media 'advertises' the lifestyle poor people might expect in richer countries. The potential devastation to the poor world of global warming and associated natural disasters, as well as increased globalisation in general, means this trend is likely to increase. This has produced increasing concerns, by some people, in terms of its effects on the social cohesion of societies, as well as the costs in benefits etc. In many countries in Europe this has led to an increase in support for right-wing, nationalist parties such as UKIP in Britain.

Test your understanding

1. What are the reasons for the decline in:

a) Birth and Fertility rates

b) Death and Infant Mortality rates.

2. What are the possible effects of higher life expectancy?

3. Summarise the changes in the nature of migration to and from /Britain over the past 30 years.

The Family, the Economy and Social Structure

Learning objectives

1. To understand the changes that have occurred in the family since industrialization
2. To understand the connections between changes in the family and economic and other social changes.
3. To analyse and assess theoretical views and models of the changing family.

There are strong relationships between the nature of the family and the economy. Marxists of course take the strongest view in this context, arguing that the relationships within, and roles of, the family are determined by the economic system, but all sociologists accept that economic factors have a considerable effect on the family. Let us examine, briefly how the family has adapted in response to economic changes.

Industrialisation

Before the Industrial Revolution (18th Century) most people lived and worked on the land. People were largely self-sufficient producing their own food, shelter etc. It used to be thought that people lived in extended families at this time but **Peter Laslett** used parish records **(a secondary, historical source)** to demonstrate that most people, in England, lived in a type of Nuclear Family. This was because the oldest son inherited property and other children had to move to get jobs. However this type of nuclear family was very different from todays. Most families maintained contact and support and, indeed, the whole community (village etc.) would help at harvest time or in building or other work. In **Durkheim's** words they led very similar lives and had similar attitudes and interests so they "stuck together" because they depended on each other – he calls this **Mechanical solidarity**

The Industrial Revolution (18th Century) produced huge changes in peoples lives. Farming became mechanised and the land was increasingly controlled by rich landowners. Poorer people lost their land and jobs. They moved to the towns (**urbanisation**) to get jobs in the new factories and mines. They became wage earners. Often these jobs involved terrible working conditions. Illness, injury and unemployment were common problems and there was no Welfare State. So families lived close to, or with, wider relatives for help and support. In these areas the **extended family** became the norm. **Anderson (1971)** demonstrate this in his study of working class family life in Preston, using evidence from the 1851 Census (official statistics) He makes the point that when people moved to the city they often moved in with wider family and then got a house nearby. Living in large family groups saved money on rent and employers often recruited staff through the family.

The 20th Century saw further, rapid economic change, with the development of new industries, especially in the service sector. This required families to become both socially and geographically mobile. **Functionalists** like **Parsons** argues that these changes resulted in the modern nuclear

29

family He sees the Nuclear family as being superior to other forms, it is functional for both society and the individual. He argues that in modern societies **status** is **achieved** rather than ascribed. The extended family with its greater controls held people back. The Nuclear family encourages its members to better themselves; to move around for better jobs and living conditions.

Parsons identifies the following features of the modern nuclear family:

Loss of functions of the family – education, healthcare etc. are taken over and done much more effectively through other institutions – The Welfare State, schools and hospitals .

The Nuclear family is small and has less dependence on wider kin and so **can move around for jobs**. This is essential in Capitalist Societies where work is always changing.

The Nuclear family can concentrate on its essential functions – socialisation of children and providing for the emotional needs of its members. The family becomes a source of calm and rest in an increasingly stressful (working) world

In other words the family **adapted** (changed) in order to be functional (meet the needs) of a new type of society (modern capitalist society).

Evaluation Parsons assumption that the modern, isolated Nuclear family evolved from the extended factory is simplistic and historically inaccurate – see Laslett (above). His analysis also seems outdated given the diversity of family forms today.

Young and Willmott – 'The Symmetrical Family'

Young and Willmott (1973) argue (from a basically Functionalist viewpoint) that the family had gone through three basic stages of development:

Stage 1 The pre-industrial family.
Before the Industrial Revolution the family was a unit of production, in other words it produced most of its own food and other needs – most families lived in the country and worked in farming.

Stage 2 The early industrial family

Developed in the 19th Century and reached its peak in the early 20th Century. People went "out to work" in the new factories etc. They earned money to buy the goods they need and live in extended family networks for mutual support (see above). Such families were mostly working class and still exist in some urban areas.

Stage 3 – The Symmetrical Family

By the 1970s the stage 2 extended family had largely disappeared. The family has become isolated and home-centred – free time is spent doing chores and leisure is largely home based – watching TV etc. Husband and wife have **joint conjugal roles**, they share responsibilities for work, housework and children and are far more equal than in the past. The family has fewer children and puts the needs of the children first i.e. it is **child-centred. Willmott and Young** argue that this new pattern of families started with the m/c and worked its way down to the w/c; they call this process stratified diffusion.

Much of their ideas were based on their study of **"Family and Kinship in East London"** (in Bethnal Green). They found that the traditional w/c, extended, **matriarchal families** (where the family was based round the mother/women) broke down when people moved out to Greenleigh – a new estate where people did not live near family and friends. If you watch TV soaps like Eastenders you can still see a fictionalised account of the old extended family – with female matriarchs like Peggy Mitchell. Such programmes are very popular – this is partly a result of people looking back with affection at a time of 'closer families and communities'.

Reasons for the rise of the symmetrical family

Less need for the support of wider kin because people were better paid and the Welfare state gave support in terms of unemployment, pensions, social security etc.

Geographical mobility – people moving for better jobs and housing.

Less children – didn't need grandma to help out as much!

Better housing and entertainment at home – leisure becomes home based

Willmott and Young found in their research that w/c families have more contact with extended family than m/c. This is supported by evidence by the **British Social Attitudes Survey (2005) Willmott** did more research in the 1980s and found that the extended family was still important to the modern nuclear family but contacts were more limited, no longer a central part of everyday life. They were however still important in times of emergency – funerals, money crises, domestic problems etc.

Where does all this leave us?

There is little doubt that Willmott and Young described an important general trend, however the real position is more complicated. Relationships between Nuclear and Extended vary enormously from "total isolation" to everyday interaction and dependence – but most families fall somewhere between these two extremes. The picture is further complicated by the growing diversity of family life (New Right theorists would say by the breakdown of the family).

Test your knowledge and understanding

1. Why did extended families develop during the industrial revolution?

2. Why did extended families decline during the 20th century/

3. What explanations do Wilmott and Young give for the development of symmetrical families?

Marriage, cohabitation and divorce

Learning objectives
1. Understanding explanations for the decline in marriage and the increase in cohabitation.
2. Knowledge and understanding of social variations in divorce rates.
3. Analysis and evaluation of explanations for the increase in divorce since the 1970s, including theoretical perspectives.

Marriage and cohabitation

There has been a significant **decline in the number of people who get married**. Marriage is now at its lowest rate since records began. In 1970 there were 400,000 marriages in Britain, today the figure is about half that. This does not however, necessarily mean a decline in family life, because at the same time as marriage has declined there has been a huge increase in the number of people **cohabiting** (living together). About a quarter of adults who are not married (aged 16-59) are cohabiting. About a third of people who cohabit eventually get married to each other, and over 60% of 'first time' cohabiters marry. Cohabiting can therefore, to a certain extent be seen as a 'trial marriage'.

How do we explain this trend?

Increase in divorce – people are no longer prepared to marry because of high divorce rates – marriage is considered to be far more risky than it was in the past.!

The **decline in religious influence (secularisation)** – thus couples who 'live together' are no longer stigmatised. Indeed there has been a general change in norms and values in society. People are far more tolerant of alternative lifestyles. Cohabitation is no longer looked down on.

Feminism has encouraged women to be more independent, 'not to rely on a man'. **Sue Sharpe's** study of changing girls' attitudes (see above) illustrates this development. Women put off marriage until an average age of thirty, but often cohabit before this.

Giddens argues that there has been a change to **serial monogamy** –, instead of being in permanent marriage/partnership with one person, many people go through a series of monogamous relationships with different partners.

The **New Right** would say this is a reflection of the decline in family values – lack of respect for vital institutions like marriage – often single mothers who are cohabiting are benefit-dependent and 'fiddle benefits' by pretending they do not have a partner.

Expense – it is estimated that the average marriage today costs about £15,000+.1 `

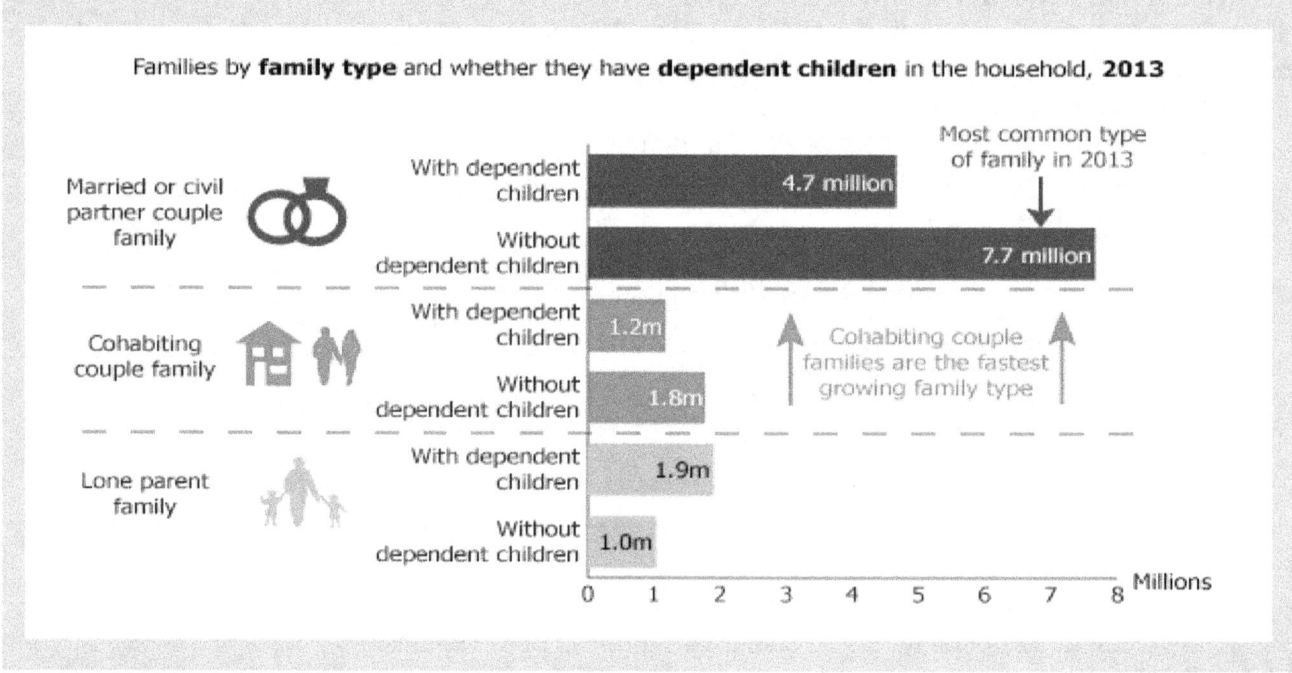

Source ONS

Divorce

Divorce can be defined as the "legal termination of a marriage". This distinguish it from when people just separate. It is not the same as marriage breakdown. This can occur when people separate or even continue to live together in **'empty shell'** marriages.

The UK has one of the highest divorce rates in Europe, though increases in divorce have occurred in all of the industrial world. In numerical terms there were 25,000 divorces in 1961, by 2005 this had risen to around 165,000. Nowadays there is about one divorce for every two marriages. The average length of marriage before divorce is about 12 years, but we should note that most people who divorce re-marry, so it is not marriage itself they reject but their particular partner (**Giddens - serial monogamy**).

Social Variations in Divorce Rates

Teenage marriages are more likely to end in divorce

Working class couples have a higher divorce rate than m/c couples

Asians have a far lower rate of divorce than the rest of the population

Marriages that are 'mixed' in terms of social class or ethnicity are more likely to end in divorce

Childless couples are more likely to divorce.

Reconstituted families/couples have higher divorce rates.

Reasons for the increase in the Divorce Rate

Legal changes -It is now far easier to get a divorce. The **Divorce Reform Act of 1969** meant that people no longer had to prove adultery, cruelty etc. to get a divorce – now they only have to establish that the marriage has "irretrievably broken down". This change resulted in an immediate and dramatic increase in divorce. However since the 1990s the rate has remained fairly constant. Indeed Governments have made divorce slightly 'less easy'. The 1999 Act increased the amount of time before divorce could proceed to18 months and introduced compulsory marriage counselling.

Feminism - Most (75%) divorce petitions are from women. The liberated, working woman of today wants her own identity and independence and demands much more from her husband in terms of marriage relationships. If this doesn't happen she divorces him.

Functionalists argue that a certain amount of divorce is functional. It allows couples to end unhappy marriages, whereas in the past this was not possible. People have higher expectations of marriage.

In the past divorce was considered shameful – especially for women. This **stigma** has been largely removed, partly due to a decline in **religious controls and beliefs** partly because the pressures of the extended family are no longer as strong. Divorce is much easier in the privatised nuclear family. (**Beck** sees this as part of the process of **individuation** – we care far more about our own happiness than that of others).

Marx once talked about Capitalism becoming characterised by a 'fetishism of commodities' where consumerism becomes an obsession and relationships become dehumanised. One could argue that in our 'throw away' society we throw away relationships that we tire of just as we throw away our 'the other stuff' we no longer want.

Divorce – Theory

Whilst **Functionalists** would regard a certain level of divorce as necessary and even functional they would regard current rates as being far too high. The **New Right** take an even more critical approach. They regard the nuclear family, with two married parents as the basic social unit in society. Cohabiting families are far more likely to break up producing single parent families with all the problems of lack of discipline and delinquency we have already examined (see Single-parent families – above). Governments should make divorce more difficult so that people do not take the easy option and live up to their responsibilities for their children and society in general.

Feminists basically see the institution of marriage, in its current form, as favouring men in terms of domestic work, childcare and power. Radical feminists in particular stress the abuse and violence, women, and their children, often suffer. Feminists argue that the ability of women, who once had to stay in abusive or 'empty-shell' marriages, to obtain a divorce is a major step forward. The fact that ¾ of divorces are initiated by women shows that it is they who get 'the raw deal' in many marriages. Cohabitation at least allows women to 'check out' relationships, without a full commitment.

33

Marriage and divorce – a comparative perspective

Divorce occurs in almost all societies in the world; for much the same reasons as it does in the west – infidelity, dissatisfaction with a partner's performance as husband or wife etc. In pre-industrial societies however there is, generally, much more pressure on husbands and wife to stay together. This is because marriage is an economic and social alliance between different families/kinship groups. **The Nuer** of the Sudan for example are a **patrilineal** society and a woman marries into her husbands family, who pay **bride-wealth** (of between 20 and 40 cattle) for the ownership of the wife's fertility and labour. A wife has to make the best of her situation because if there is a divorce the bride-wealth will have to be repaid. However do not think that divorce is necessarily quicker and easier in our society than in others. A Hopi Indian would know that his wife had divorced him if he returned to find his belongings put outside of the front door!

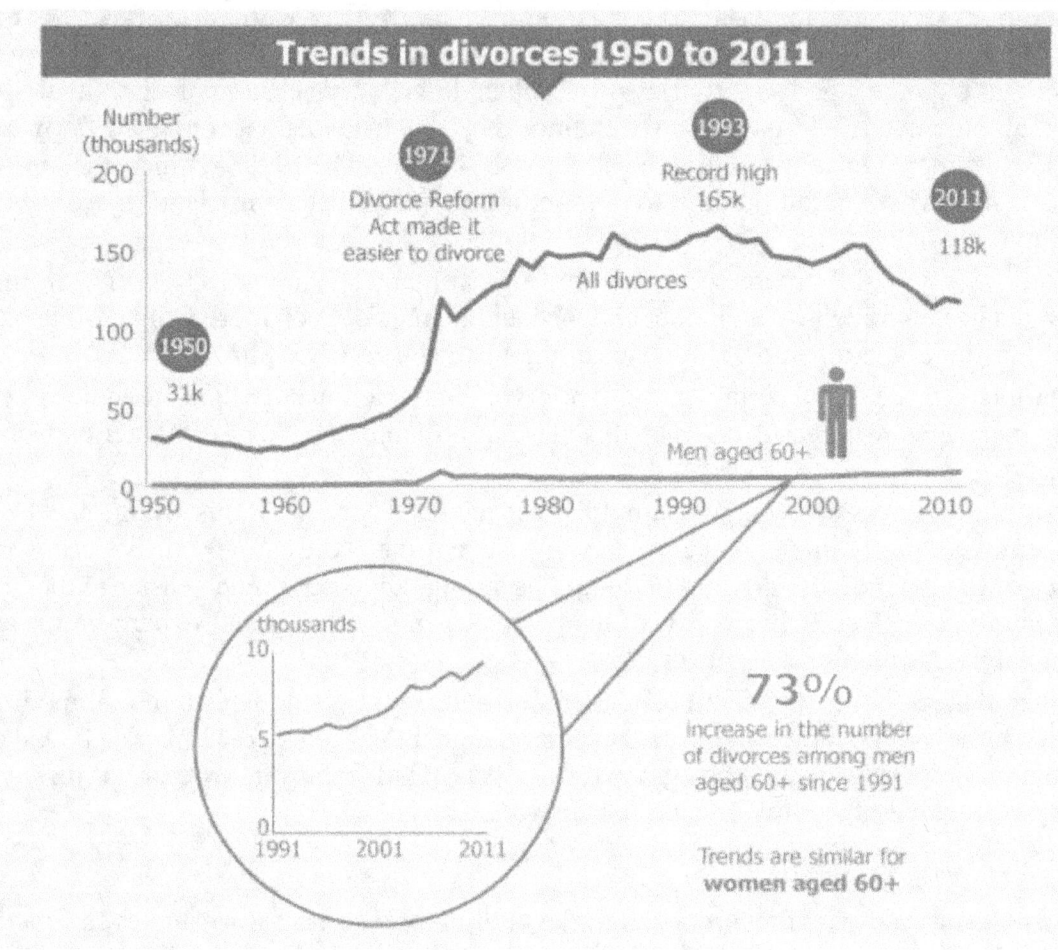

Test your knowledge and understanding

1. Outline the reasons for the decline in marriage and the increase in cohabitation. What are the connections between these changes?

2. Examine some of the reasons for social variations in Divorce Rates.

3. List the reasons for increases in divorce rates, in what you consider to be their order of importance

Roles and relationships within the family

Learning objectives

1. Knowledge and understanding of the arguments for and against the view that the gender division of labour in the home is becoming more equal. Assessment of the arguments and evidence.

2. Knowledge and understanding of nature of decision making in the home/family. Assessment of arguments and evidence

3. Analysis and evaluation of sociological theories of gender inequalities in the home.

4. Understanding and evaluation of the nature of domestic violence, and explanations of domestic violence.

Domestic labour, childcare and working women

As we have seen **Willmott and Young (1973)** argued that the modern family would be **symmetrical** and characterized **by joint conjugal roles**. In other words husband and wife would share responsibilities for childcare and housework, and power within the family would be much more equally divided.

In a previous, classic study **Bott (1957**) argued that there were two basic ways of organising husband wife relationships:

Separate conjugal roles - where the husband goes out to work does the DIY etc. and the wife does the housework, cooking and childcare.

Joint conjugal roles - where roles are more flexible – women may go out to work, men help with childcare. Also decision-making is shared, as are leisure activities.

Like Willmott and Young Bott thought that joint conjugal roles would be more typical in the modern nuclear family – partly because there would be less help from wider kin (extended family) and partly because with more women working husbands would need to help out more. Willmott and Young's research was heavily criticized by a young **Marxist-Feminist Anne Oakley.** She criticised Willmott and Young's methodology. They used a questionnaire and came up with the result that '70% of men helped with the housework". They did not look at the time men spent on housework.

Oakley's more in depth analysis, using interviews, found that:

1. Men did far less housework than women.

2. M/c men tended to help out more than w/c men.

3. Men tended to pick the housework they wanted to do! (the easy stuff).

4. In effect women took on a **dual burden** – paid work and domestic work.

Subsequent research does show a movement towards greater equality in the home, but this development has been both patchy and limited. Let us examine some of the evidence

Ferri and Smith (1996) found that 80% of women in their sample were responsible for the laundry and 66% for cleaning and cooking. Women were also far more likely to be responsible for childcare. The man was the main carer in only 4% of the families studied. – note all the women in this study were working full time and suffered from the '**dual-burden'** of full time work and housework.

Lydia Morris (1990) studied families in which the husband was unemployed and the wife worked. One would expect men in such situations to do more to 'help out'. However Morris found that the men did little more round the house than when they had been employed – possibly reflecting the

men's feeling that unemployment had been a blow to their male role as provider, and that housework would further undermine their masculinity.

35

Man-Yee Can (2001) found that women who worked full time were responsible for, on average, 65% of household chores – an improvement but far from equality. She also found (echoing Oakley) that professional couples (with degrees) shared housework much more equally than other social groups.

A study by **Gillian Dunne (1999)** found that domestic roles were far more equal amongst Lesbian couples.

All these studies, however, used small samples, so how representative are they? Much larger samples are used by the **British Social Attitudes Survey**. In a study of 1000 married couples **(2008)** the BSAS found a very clear division of labour. Women still did the vast majority of housework – for example washing and ironing was mainly done by women in 77% of households, mainly by men in 3%! Moreover 68% of women say that they 'always or usually do the cleaning'. However the BSAS did find that men did more of the 'jobs around the house' DIY and repairs etc., and that there was a general trend towards greater equality.

Power in the home

The other key area for consideration is the question of power in the household. Traditionally, of course, the male provider tended to control the finances. Typically he gave his wife the "housekeeping money" and kept the rest for himself. Thus women had the responsibility for buying food, clothes rent etc. with no power over how much money they were given. Men made the decisions.

Has this changed?

Edgell's study in the 1980s (again using a small sample of m/c couples) would suggest not. Edgell found that men made the major decisions – buying a new house or car, whilst women made the minor ones.

Jan Pahl made a series of studies of financial arrangements in the family **in the 1990s**. There were many different ways of organizing finances. In poor families the husband often gave his wife a fixed amount to manage. Frequently this meant the wife, and sometimes children "went without" whilst the husband was better off. She found the most common form of arrangement was "husband controlled pooling", in other words money is shared but the husband has the dominant role in deciding how it was spent. The least common arrangement was where women controlled spending.

Anne Oakley makes an interesting point. Most of us assume that men have always been the provider, women the housewife. In actual fact the housewife role was a product of Industrialisation it was socially constructed. Before the Industrial Revolution most people worked from home and women were a vital part of this **Domestic Economy.** It is only as industrialization developed and people went **out** to work that women began to be the one's that stayed at home to perform the mother/housewife role. This lessened their power and influence as compared to husbands.

Explaining gender inequalities in the family

1. For **Functionalists** different gender roles are natural and revolve around the fact that women are child bearers and so tied to the home for significant periods. The man as main provider and woman as housewife mother is the most effective way of keeping the family, and society ordered and stable.

2. For **Marxists** the separate, and unequal roles of men and women in the family demonstrate the power of capitalism to control family life. Even though more women work (often for low pay) capitalism still needs them to perform the "nurturing, caring role" to ensure that workers are kept fit, happy and healthy (and to prepare the next generation of workers). Hence traditional female roles and virtues are emphasized by the Ideological State Apparatus – the media, school etc.

3. **Feminists** similarly emphasise women's lack of power. Their role is still secondary to the man. The family is one of the ways in which male dominance (Patriarchy) is passed from generation to generation, through language, toys and the different ways boys and girls are treated. Women are

brought up to be passive and men to be assertive. Men may feel that their masculinity is threatened if they don't make the decisions.

4. **Postmodernists and 'Personal Life'** theorists argue that inequalities are decreasing and that now gender relationships are more a question of negotiation and choice and previously established structures and roles are breaking down.

Domestic Violence

One of the major criticisms of the Functionalist view of the family is that it ignores the violence and abuse that has always been a part of family life. It is still difficult to establish the exact extent of domestic violence. The family is a private place, and is very difficult to study – especially on sensitive issues like this that people want to keep hidden. We thus have little idea of the level of abuse and violence in the past, though what is true is that violence to both women, and children was considered far more more socially acceptable in the past. .Canes and straps were often used to punish children and many people accepted that a man had the right to "punish" his wife if she was "out of line" (some still do today!).

The official figures tell us that 1 in 3 cases of all reported violence is domestic and reported by women. Again we must be careful, most domestic violence is not reported. Some studies have also shown an increase in female violence towards their male partners, but at most this probably constitutes around 5% of domestic violence.

The classic study of domestic violence was carried out by **Dobash and Dobash (1992).** They found that Official Statistics seriously underestimated the amount of Domestic violence. For their study, in Glasgow, they used structured and unstructured interviews to get both "the figures" and the "feelings" of the women who suffered from domestic violence. The study was both in depth and highly valid. They found that;

"Violence was used by the men they lived with to silence them, to win arguments, to express dissatisfaction, to deter future behaviour and to express dominance"

Radical Feminists argue that the police treat domestic violence differently to other forms of violence and although the police have improved procedures conviction rates are very low. This is also because women who are "battered" feel guilty, ashamed and stigmatised – this is part of **Patriarchal Ideology** – the idea that women should "know their place" and that the violence women suffer is a result of their own inadequacies as a wife. Indeed Dobash and Dobash found that most victims returned to their abusive partners because of fear of being stigmatised and because of their financial dependence on their partner.

Evaluation

Functionalists argue that Feminists place too much emphasis on violence in the family and ignore the fact that most families offer caring and loving environments. **Feminists** are also accused of ignoring female domestic violence and of treating women as powerless victims; this is patronizing to women. Women increasingly have power within the family and Post-modernists emphasize the choice and control women now have – they can leave and start again.

Test your understanding

1. What is the difference between joint and separate conjugal roles?

2. What arguments did sociologists put forward to support the view that gender roles in the household were becoming more equal?

3. Summarize, in a chart, the evidence for and against the view that gender roles in the home are becoming more equal.

4. To what extent does sociological evidence support the view that decision making in the family of today is more equal.

5. How do Functionalist and Feminist views of inequalities in gender roles in the home differ?

6. What explanations do sociologists give for domestic violence? Why is domestic violence such a difficult subject to study?

Childhood

Learning objectives

1. Understanding of why sociologists regard childhood as a **social construct.**

2. Knowledge and understanding of changes in the nature and experience of childhood since the 19th Century.

3. Assessment of explanations of changes in childhood.

4. Understanding and assessment of positive and negative views of the experience of childhood in the UK today.

5. Knowledge and understanding of the experience of childhood in other societies.

6. Understanding and evaluation of theories of childhood and the future of childhood.

Sociologists argue that childhood is not just a biological stage of development but a **social construct**. The idea that children differ from adults in terms of behaviour, attitudes, rights etc. is not the same everywhere in the world. Nor was it true in the past. In many, if not most, societies in the world children work from an early age. Traditionally in 'peasant' societies they will work on the land with their mothers and fathers. In the developing world many children now work in factories or workshops from the age of 6 or 7. They are, of course, paid minimum wages.

Airies claimed that the concept of childhood in Western societies was only developed comparatively recently. In pre-industrial societies children were treated as "small adults" with no special rights. They took part in the same work, and play as adults. Children were regarded more as an economic asset than beloved offspring. In medieval times they worked on the land, in the early Industrial Revolution in the mines and factories, often from the age of six or seven. Airies based some of his research on medieval pictures that showed children as "mini-adults" – same clothes, even same proportions. Children were also promised in marriage at an early age (especially by Monarchs and the Aristocracy - big landowners), in order to gain territory and forge alliances. It should be remembered that the conditions at this time meant that attitudes to children had to be different – over a third died at an early age; life (especially for the poor) was "nasty, brutish and short".

There have been criticisms of Aires. Archaeological finds have shown beautifully crafted toys from the most ancient of times, and written sources also show that children were, to some extent regarded as special. However their can be little doubt that the very special treatment and protection of children that is common today is really an invention of the late 20th Century.

Attitudes started to change in the 19th Century when children were banned from working in the mines and factories. However child abuse, prostitution and crime were common through most of the 19th century. The introduction of compulsory education was another key moment (1870) though this was more about economic needs of society than the interests of the child.

The 20th century is sometimes called "the century of the child". As living standards improved and death rates fell the family became more child-centred. Children now went to school and were no longer a source of income. This meant people began to have fewer children (in the knowledge they were far more likely to survive). The increased availability of effective contraception allowed people to plan their families. All these developments enabled parents to invest more time, love and protection in their children. Children were thus seen as in need of special care and attention.

A Child-centred Society?

Over the past 50 years the state has increasingly intervened to support children and their rights. It is

38

argued that societies like Britain have become **'child-centred'**. Let us examine some of these changes, and there causes:

The decline in child mortality meant that parents were able to have fewer children and be fairly certain that they would survive. These fewer children could be given better material conditions (food, housing, clothes etc.) and also more love and attention.

Compulsory education from the 1870s, children could no longer work from an early age and this distinguished them from adults – made them 'different'. Educational reforms have also increased the amount of time that children are dependent on their parents. Today most young people stay on in education or training until they are at least 18.

The types of **jobs** young people can do as well as working hours, and the ages at which children can work (13) are tightly controlled by law. **Children are no longer a source of income, but an expensive proposition**, largely dependent on their parents to provide them with the vast array of consumer goods aimed at children (another recent development). Consumer goods, media programmes and formats, and advertising are specifically targeted at children (and teenagers) taking advantage of young peoples **'pester power'**. There have been increasing concerns about, for example, the advertising of fatty foods and the violence contained in many computer games. There has even been some legislation preventing the advertising of unhealthy foods at peak children's TV viewing times.

Laws against cruelty to children (the first in 1889), and recognising the rights of children have been passed throughout the last century. **The Child Support Act (1991)**, for example, deals with the care, upbringing and protection of children and in the event of family break up and has given more voice to children and their needs.

Specialist Doctors, Social Workers and other professionals protect and support children (and families) at risk; whether it be from ill health, poverty or abuse. **Child benefits, Family tax credits** and other policies like **'Sure Start'** are all designed to support children – especially the disadvantaged.

Age restrictions on children also reflect societies view that childhood is a distinct phase in human life when young people are not sufficiently mature to make certain decisions for themselves. Children are not allowed to buy alcohol until they are 18, they cannot drive until they are seventeen, or vote until they are 18. I'm sure you can think of many other examples.

The 'dark side' of childhood

Child abuse. We must be careful how we define "abuse" because it can vary from violence and sex abuse to various degrees of neglect. Is the family that give their children junk food and make them obese guilty of child abuse? Despite the media's publicity re paedophiles it is a sad fact **that most child abuse happens within the family**. Most sociologists and psychologists see child abuse as a question of power. It is more common in step families and amongst those (mostly men) who have themselves been abused. Children often find it difficult to report abuse because of the private nature of the family and fear – both of the abuser and of the consequences for the family. It is also difficult to get convictions in court. Child abuse is often seen as a growing problem but it is more likely that more abuse is now discovered. Organisations such as **Child-line** provide a means of children seeking help. We should also remember that what might now be defined as child abuse e.g. violence towards children would once have been regarded as socially acceptable – caning, and the use of the leather strap to beat children are two examples.

Bullying – especially in schools. Again this is seen as a growing problem but in reality this is largely the result of changing perception as to what bullying is. Bullying is now defined as emotional and social as well as physical. As schools have set up counselling systems so more bullying has been reported.

Protection as abuse. Frank Ferudi (Paranoid Parenting 2001) argues constant moral panics about stranger danger, pedophilia, youth gangs, drugs etc have led parents to adopt an over-protective attitude towards children. Governments have encouraged this by their insistence on 'vetting' all adults who work with children. Parents no longer trust their own judgment and try to

39

protect their children by control of their movements and activities. This means that they miss out on the freedom childhood should involve and do not gain the experience of managing risk that is an essential skill in childhood.

Consumerism as abuse Some sociologists argue that as business and the mass media have increasingly targeted children as a lucrative market, so parents have given children more and more 'goodies' – toys, computer games, designer clothes etc. some parents who work long hours use this as compensation for the limited time they spend with their children.

Public Domain Image

Childhood – international perspectives

Childhood is a very different experience amongst the poor of the developing world. In some ways the experience of such children is similar to that of children during the Industrial Revolution in Britain. Children are a source of labour and income, for poor families and often education is cut short so that children can work alongside their parents on the land or in the factories and workshops. Poverty and exploitation are common. In many developing countries there are few laws to protect children from exploitation. We should also note that such children are often indirectly employed by British and Western firms. Companies like Nike, Primark and Gap, amongst many others, have been accused of profiting from child labour.

Research Study: The Townsend Centre for International Poverty Research.

This huge survey used secondary data from 46 developing countries. It makes depressing reading:

1. Over 1/3 of children in developing countries suffer from absolute poverty.
2. Over 1/3 of children live in housing where there are five or more people to one room.
3. One in 7 children have never attended school.
4. As many as 1/3 have no close access to clean water supplies.

Children in developing countries often suffer from **poor health and high mortality rates**. Malnutrition, dirty water and infectious diseases take a terrible toll. Besides diseases like malaria and diarrhea, millions of children have been orphaned by the AIDs epidemic. Millions are HIV positive.

Children, in developing countries may also be sold into prostitution and even slavery. In areas of civil war such as Uganda, the Congo and Sudan children are 'recruited' (forced) to become soldiers, and often witness or take parting acts of murder and torture.

Study Small Wars (1991)– Donna Goldstein

Goldstein did an ethnographic study of a family who lived in a Favella (shanty town) in Rio De Janeiro, Brazil. Like many poor families Gracia (the mother) was a single parent, coping, on her own, with 13 children in a small two-room slum. Her children were expected to work from a very

40

early age – often helping mum to clean the houses of the rich, and were subject to discipline that we would see as child abuse. However Garcia's main concern was to keep her children away from the criminal (drugs) gangs who dominate the Favella. She did not want them to join such gangs, many of whose members die in their teenage years. To do this she thought the children had to be more frightened of her than of the gangs.

Goldstein describes the terrible condition such children have to live with. Many live on the streets from a very early age. Girls are forced into prostitution, boys into drugs and stealing, there are few legitimate job opportunities. These young street children are also subject to violence. Many are killed by gangs and the police.

Theory and research

Both **Functionalists** and the **New Right** tend to take a "conventional approach" to childhood. They argue that 2 parent families are vital for care and socialisation. **Charles Murray**, as we have seen, argues that welfare dependency has led to increased crime and deviance amongst the underclass and a lack of respect for authority. Children are socialised into these anti-social values and a 'yob culture' has developed. Single parent families and high divorce rates are undermining the family and society. Children are seen as 'victims' of these processes as family influence declines so that of peers and the media grows. **Melanie Phillips** argues that "liberal" attitudes mean that children do not have enough respect for parents. They are increasingly under media pressure to "grow up too fast" and, particularly girls, to become sexual beings at an increasingly early age. Thus the innocence of childhood is lost.

Neil Postman is a key figure in this debate. In '**The Death of Childhood**'(1994) he argues that children are growing up too fast. Children wear adult clothes, and can access adult material on the internet. The rate of teenage pregnancies has dramatically increased as under-age sex has become more and more common.

Marxists (guess what?) argue that capitalism, and the consumerism it encourages, sees children as a lucrative market. Parents are encouraged to spend more and more money on children, but often give them less time **(Seabrook).** Material spoiling is accompanied by emotional neglect.

Other views are less pessimistic. **Morrow's research (1998)** found that children could make sense of and contribute to their own family lives. Children did not want to make their own decisions but they did want a say in family life

It is also important to remember that experiences of childhood vary enormously in Britain
Social class is very important. Middle class children tend to benefit from their cultural and material advantages. They do better at school etc. Working class and Underclass children are more likely to suffer from poverty and ill health.

Experiences also vary according to **ethnicity.** There is evidence that Moslem, Hindu and Sikh children tend to feel greater obligations to parents and so "the generation gap" is not so apparent. However the culture clash such children may feel can have other results e.g. S. Asian girls are 3 time more likely to commit suicide than white girls.

Gender also has its effects. Girls tend to be more controlled than boys by parents, and boys and girls are still socialised into different gender roles and norms.

We should also remember those children who suffer from **neglect and abuse** – there are over 30,000 children on child protection registers, and these are only those that are known about.

Test your knowledge and understanding

1. Why is it wrong to see childhood as a purely a question of age?

2. What evidence does Airies use to support his claim that childhood is a social construct?

3. How have demographic changes improved the quality of childhood?

4. Outline some of the ways in which changes in the law have benefited children.

5. Examine the problems sociologists face in defining and measuring child abuse.

6. In what ways can 'spoiling children' be seen as a form of neglect or abuse?

7. What does Ferudi mean when he says children today are over-protected?

8. What arguments and evidence do some sociologists put forward to support the 'death of childhood' thesis?

9. What social variations are there in the experience of childhood?

10. Outline some of the problems that children in developing countries face

Family Policy

Learning Objectives
1. Knowledge and understanding of a range of policies and legislation affecting the family.
2. Knowledge and understanding of contemporary Labour and Conservative family policies.
3. Knowledge and understanding of family policy in other societies.
4. Analysis and evaluation of theoretical perspectives on family policy

By Family Policy we mean the laws and policies that Governments devise that relate to the family issues examples include divorce laws, child protection laws and benefits (financial) aimed at supporting the family.

A wide range of policies have been brought in since WW2 the past 50 years, that have had a considerable impact on family life. These include:

The establishment of the original 'Welfare State' after WW2. This was the basis of family policy for many years. It included measures such as full-time secondary education for all, a National Health Service, and action against poverty – including unemployment pay, state pensions for the retired and other benefits. All these policies supported the family, both directly and indirectly.

The legalization of abortion and availability of free contraception (from the 1960s).

Easier Divorce (1970s) onwards.

Equal Pay and Sex Discrimination Acts (1979) which encouraged women to go out to work and attempted to establish equal opportunities.

The rights of children have also been improved by a series of Children's Acts. These include measures to protect vulnerable children and social workers dedicated to supporting the family.

Conservative Family Policy in the 1980s and 90s.
Until the end of the 1990s, particularly under the **Conservative Governments of Margaret Thatcher and John Major,** there was a strong **'ideological' commitment to the two-parent nuclear family** (as there had been since the war). But, as we have seen, times were changing and the diversity of family lifestyles was growing. Taking a '**New Right'** approach lone parent families were condemned and Major launched a (doomed) campaign called 'Back to Basics' which called for a return to 'traditional family values'. The **Child Support Agency** was also established (1991) which aimed to force 'fathers' to pay maintenance and thus cut the amount of welfare payments to single-mothers. There were also legislative attempts to cut divorce rates – again unsuccessfully.

Labour Family Policy 1997-2010
The '**New' Labour** government showed signs of a shift in policy towards a greater tolerance towards 'unconventional family types. Whilst supporting marriage and the nuclear family they had not wanted to be seen as 'interfering in people's family choices'. 'New Labour', under **Tony Blair,** can be best summed up by Blair's statement that the policy was '**Work for those who can, security for those that can't'** (again there is a New Right influence here).

> **Measures**
>
> **The New Deal** – was designed to encourage people to 'get off the welfare' and into employment. In particular lone mothers were targeted. Since 2001 all lone parents have been required to attend an annual assessment interview to assess work prospects.
>
> **'Sure Start'** which provides more support for women with children, especially single parents, encouraging them to go to work.
>
> Dealing with **Child Poverty** has been a major concern. Improved child benefits, payable to the mother, were increased by 26% in real terms between 1997 and 2002 – taking 600,000 children out of poverty. However between 2005 and 2008 child poverty figures began to rise again.
>
> The Labour Government brought in **Family Tax Credit**, which, by topping up the incomes of poor working families, made them better off – and also tried to encourage more poorer people to work.

Conservative/Coalition Family Policy today

Since the 2010 General Election the Coalition Government has focused like governments before it on 'getting people off benefits and back to work'. Housing benefit cuts and the cap on benefits (of £26,000 maximum) means that those who live in areas where rents are expensive or in large families are likely to suffer hardship. Critics also argue that scrapping child benefit for couples where one parent earns more than £42,475, but not when both parents each earn just under that sum, is extremely unfair. The Conservative victory in the 2015 General Election was immediately followed by proposals to further cut welfare benefits by £12 billion – mostly by limiting housing benefits and family tax credits available to low paid workers.

Family Policy – International perspectives.

All societies have laws and policies that affect the family. Demographic, economic, social and political factors are all influential. In China and India, for example, the huge population increases of the 20th century produced family policies, very much based on reducing population growth. In China a **'one child'** policy, which provided tax and other incentives for parents who only had one child, has had significant effects in this respect. There has been considerable political pressure on families to adopt the policy and use both birth control and abortion to reduce family size (critics argue that this amounts to force and is a human rights issue). In **India** the approach has been based more on education and persuasion (and sometimes bribery). It has achieved some success, though not as much as in China. The small state of **Kerala** in Southern India, however, has had astonishing success in this area. Here the State Government focused on improving medical care and reducing infant mortality, whilst at the same time encouraging contraception and providing universal education. Couples were thus persuaded to have less children because they knew that there, fewer, children were likely to survive, and that as parents they could provide better care

In contrast to this **Communist Russia** encouraged people to have more children in the 1950s (the Russian population had been decimated by WW2). Women who had 5 children or more were given medals! The 'Communist' societies of Eastern Europe provided comprehensive, if often basic, welfare systems. When Communism fell and a free market was introduce many poorer people and pensioners suffered from the decline in welfare support.

Family Policy – Theoretical perspectives

Functionalists, in general supported welfare policies such as the Welfare State. Parsons argued that welfare support – education, health etc allowed the nuclear family to specialise in its two key functions – socialisation and the stabilisation of adult personalities (see above). Easier divorce can also be seen as functional, as it allows dysfunctional ' broken marriages' to be ended. Since the late 1970s Functionalist theory has declined in influence and the New Right has become the predominant 'conservative' sociological perspective.*The New Right* argue that, easier divorce abortion etc have undermined the family. The increased number of women working means they are less committed to the family, and children suffer from maternal deprivation. State benefits have

43

encouraged single mums and fathers who take no responsibility for their children. The growth of the benefit dependent **underclass,** who socialise their children into a culture of crime and antisocial behaviour, is the key problem facing family life and society in general. Abortion on demand and the legalisation of homosexuality also show a moral decline. The New Right advocate cuts in benefit payments and welfare measures to get people back to work and off benefits. Their ideas have influenced both Conservative and Labour Governments (policies like the 'New Deal' etc)

Feminists tend to approve of policies that have improved the rights of women such as easier abortion and divorce, (which feminists campaigned strongly for). However they criticise government family policy for its continued commitment to a '**Family Ideology'** that focuses on the Nuclear Family as being the ideal – ignoring growing family diversity. This **patriarchal** ideology of the family is reinforced by the media, politicians, religion and schools; so we have a situation where even though most women work, they are still expected to be mainly responsible for housework and childcare – not to mention caring for elderly relatives etc (**dual or even triple burden**). Policies such as increased maternity leave are also criticised. They reinforce the view that women are responsible for childcare. The Labour Government responded to this by increasing Paternity leave.

Marxists have argued that welfare policies, including family policy, reflects the needs of capitalism. Education and Healthcare help to ensure a healthy and trained workforce. The increase in women working, often in low paid jobs, provides an easily exploited workforce. The low pensions paid to the (poor) old are also criticised. **Lasch** argues that these reflect the fact that old people do not work and so are considered 'useless' in the Capitalist system.. Some Neo-Marxists, however, argue that improvements in w/c life are the result of the struggles of working people to improve the quality of their lives. **Marxists and feminists** also criticise policy on domestic violence and child abuse. These are huge problems because the State sees the family as a private institution and does not like to interfere.

Test your knowledge and understanding

1. In what ways did the establishment of the Welfare State provide support for the family?

2. How have Conservative policies on the family changed, since the 1990s?

3. Outline the main features of Labour Party Family Policy since 1997.

4. What criticisms do the New Right make of Family Policy?

What criticisms do Marxists and Feminists make of Family Policy?

AS and A-Level Exam Questions and Tips

AS Exam type questions

(*The AS paper has three short questions worth two, two and six marks, examples below:*

1. Define the term nuclear family. (2 marks)

2. Define the term instrumental role. (2 marks)

3. Define the term cohabitation. (2 marks)

(*These are obviously basic knowledge and understanding questions. You should not write too much, just try to give a clear definition*)

4. Using one example explain how immigration may effect family diversity in Britain. (2 marks)

5. Using one example explain how the reduction in the birth rate may have affected roles in the family. (2 marks)

44

6. Using one example explain how changes in the law may have affected the experience of childhood in Britain. (2 marks)

(Again these questions require short answers. For example in Q4 you could say that 'Immigration from the West Indies has increased the number of (female) single parent families because there are a higher proportion of such families in The West Indies' That is enough for two marks.)

7. Outline three reasons for the increase in the divorce rate over the past 50 years. (6 marks)

8. Outline three reasons for the increase in women taking part in paid employment over the past 50 years. (6 marks)

9. Outline three reasons for the decrease in the birth rate over the past 100 years, (6 marks)

(These questions require brief explanations. You don't have to explain in detail, after all it's only 2 marks for each reason. Take Q7 for example:

'The law has made it easier for people to get divorced – you don't have to prove cruelty etc, just irretrievable breakdown of marriage' would be more than enough to give you 2 marks.

AS and A-Level Questions

(There are no short questions on the family in the A-Level paper – just two 10 mark and one 20 mark questions. The AS paper has one 10 mark and one 20 mark question – following the three short questions. Both papers have the 'outline and explain' question, examples of which are to be found below)

1. Outline and explain two ways in which the family has become more diverse in the last thirty years. (10 marks)

2. Outline and explain two ways in which women's increased involvement in paid work has affected family structures. (10 marks)

3. Outline and explain two ways in which society has become more 'child-centred' over the past 100 years (10 marks)

(This question obviously requires some depth and detail. For example in Q1 you would first have to identify a factor ' There are more single parent families' for example, and then explain why - ' The increase in the divorce rate and the number of unmarried women having babies has meant that the number of 'single parent families has significantly increased. The most important reason is the increase in divorce. In 1970 divorce became both easier to obtain, and cheaper. Divorce rates immediately rose to much higher levels. Changing attitudes are also important, being a single-parent was once considered a source of shame, now there is far less stigma attached. The decline in traditional religious influence (secularisation) is part of the explanation for this, as is changing attitudes influenced by Feminist ideas. The growth of the Welfare State has enabled single parents to survive more easily by providing a range of benefits. Women no longer have to rely on a man to provide for them. Thus there are now substantially more single parent families – mostly headed by women and this has significantly added to the diversity of the family'

A-Level questions

(The second question on the full A-Level question is also a 10 mark question. This does not appear on the AS paper. You will be given a short extract of material to apply in your answer. You should develop points from this not just repeat it. The question will be worded:

'Applying material from Item A:'

1. Analyse two reasons for the increase in single-parent families in Britain. (10 marks)

2. Analyse two ways in which the experience of childhood has changed in Britain over the past 100 years. (10 marks)

45

3. Analyse two changes in the roles of women in the family over the past 50 years. (10 marks)

Note. When asked to analyse you need to identify two reasons and then explain them in some detail, you should also try to evaluate some of the points made. Look at the following example (answering Q3) to see how this is done:

'Item A asserts that the reduction in family size, partly facilitated by improved family planning and better contraception, has meant women can now spend far less of their time looking after children. The average number of children in a family has fallen to around two in the 21st century. This means they can engage in paid employment and pursue a career far more easily than they could in the past. The provision of maternity (and paternity) leave, with pay, is also helpful in this context. Feminists argue that this has also enabled women to become more independent and play a significant role in providing family income, thus enabling greater equality between husband and wife and empowering women. Women can also devote more resources and time to the (fewer) children they have and the modern 'child-centered' family can, according to Functionalists, thus more easily provide for the material and expressive needs of all its members.

However Feminists argue there is a downside to this. Though women have less children they are still expected to take most of the responsibility for childcare and society expects children to be given far more attention than in the past. Feminists also argue that greater gender equality in the family is exaggerated. It is still women who do most of the housework and, indeed, with the increase in life expectancy are often faced with the 'triple- burden' of housework, childcare (and 'husband-care!) and looking after elderly parents.

Note how, in this answer. The first paragraph analyses and explains the change and the second paragraph evaluates the change by looking at the 'other side of the argument'. You should attempt to do this in your answers to this type of question.

AS and A-Level Question – the Essay

In both the AS and A-Level the final family question is an essay worth 20 marks. The essay is an evaluation question. Note that when asked to evaluate you are required to examine and explain evidence, arguments etc on both (or more!) sides of the argument. To attain high grades analysis and evaluation are essential. Again you will be given some stimulus material which you need to use by developing points from it. The wording of the question will be:

'Applying material from the Item and your knowledge...'

1. Evaluate the view that, in the family today, people choose and negotiate what forms their relationships will take. (20 marks)

2. Evaluate the view that the division of labour and power relationships in couples are equal in modern family life. (20 marks)

3. Evaluate the contribution of Functionalist views to our understanding of the family.

Note that Q3 is a good example of a theory essay. You might alternatively be asked to evaluate Marxist or Feminist contributions.

When approaching such essays an essay plan outlining the main points you wish to develop is a good idea. In Q3 you will need to explain the theories/functions outlined by Murdock, Parsons etc. You would then need to evaluate these theories by using other views e.g. Marxist, Feminist, New Right etc. Note evaluation can be both positive and critical. When evaluating try to do so on a point by point basis, not by 'writing all that Functionalists have to say and then what there critics say'. Here is an example:

'Functionalists argue that one of the main functions of the family is to provide stable sexual relationships for adults and control the sexual behaviour of its members. The fact that the values and norms of society support sexual relationships between husband and wife helps to

prevent jealousy, illegitimacy and conflict. New Right theorists would support this view but argue that with increased family breakdown the family is no longer providing this function effectively. Feminists would argue that the family system only tends to control and regulate women's sexual behaviour and represses their freedom.....'

Note that, as well as an explanation of the function (analysis) there are two evaluation points here. Other functions should be similarly explained and analysed and, where possible, evaluated.

TOPIC 2: EDUCATION

What is education?

> **Learning objectives**
>
> 1. Understanding of why compulsory education was introduced in Britain.
>
> 2. Knowledge and understanding of an outline history of education since 1870.

A simple definition of education is "Learning". It is a process that continues throughout a person's life. What we usually mean by education is, however, a bit more specific – we think of schools, colleges, universities etc. This is in fact **Formal education** where learning is organised and carried out by specialists - teachers. We also learn through **Informal education**. In fact most of what we learn we "pick up" from those around us and we may not even be aware that we are learning.

Exercise: Think of examples of how we learn "informally" and those we learn from.

Formal education is, of course, part of the socialisation process – secondary socialisation. As we will see success in education is heavily dependent on how well we are prepared in the primary stage of socialisation.

Formal education is a relatively new thing as far as ordinary people are concerned. Before Industrialisation only the elite were educated – in private schools or by private tutors. In Pre-industrial societies education came from family and peers who taught children what they needed to know for life – hunting, farming, crafts etc. – this is still the case in pre-industrial societies today.

As the Industrial Revolution developed, however, there was a greatly increased **division of labour**– a much greater variety of jobs, and a more skilled and educated workforce was needed to do them.

> **Compulsory education, for all was therefore introduced in Britain, in 1870, for several reasons :-**
>
> . Most importantly, to provide a workforce with the necessary skills for economic success against Britain's competitors like Germany, who already had a compulsory system.
>
> . To control the masses. Education encouraged patriotism and respect for those at the top. (more and more **men** were getting the vote those at the top wanted to make sure they voted for the right people – them!).
>
> . Some reformers genuinely wanted to help the poor improve themselves through education.

A brief history of Education in Britain

Up until the late 19th century state education hardly existed. Of course there had always been private education – mostly for the higher social classes – and some poorer children received basic schooling provided by the church and charities, but most children only received education from their families. It was not formal education, but the learning of 'life skills' in other words how to survive as a poor person in a very unequal society.

The Forster Act (1870) introduced compulsory education at Elementary (Primary) level. The 20th Century saw a gradual increase in Secondary education though this mostly benefited middle class pupils as most pupils had to pay.

The Butler Act 1944. Established the **Tripartite System**. Pupils took an 11+ exam to decide whether they went to Grammar, Technical or Secondary Modern schools. Selection was supposed to be on the basis of ability.

1960s –The start of **Comprehensive Education** as a response to the inequalities of the Tripartite system. Sociologists had found that working class children were at a great disadvantage.

Comprehensives would take in all pupils irrespective of background or ability. So equality of opportunity would be established and success would be based on ability –**Meritocracy.**

1980s and 90s Numerous reforms based on Conservative policies of introducing competition to schools to improve standards, the **Marketisation of education** – Vocational Education, National Curriculum etc.

1997 onwards the Labour Government, and subsequent Coalition Govt continued some Conservative policies – but, in the case of Labour, with more emphasis on dealing with social exclusion and improving achievement of (lower) w/c and ethnic minorities pupils and increasing the numbers of students in Higher Education.

A Victorian School – Public Domain Image

Test your understanding

Look again at the reasons why compulsory education was introduced in 1870. How are the roles of education today similar and different?

Education – theories/perspectives

Learning objectives
1. Knowledge and understanding of sociological theories of education.
2. Knowledge and understanding of related concepts, studies and research
3. Analysis, comparison and evaluation of different sociological theories of education.

Functionalism

The Functionalist perspective dominated the Sociology of Education until the 1970s. As we have seen Functionalists argue that society is based on agreed values (value consensus). Because people share the same basic values, norms and beliefs, they want similar things in life. The Education System is one of the institutions that socialises people into the norms and values of society. It also teaches the skills and knowledge that society needs, and which enables individuals to be successful members of society.

Functionalists examine the **functions of education i.e. the part played by education in producing a stable, healthy, ordered, society.** They have an essentially positive view of education.

Emile Durkheim argued that education was a "mirror to society". In other words the education system reflects the values, norms etc of society as a whole and functions to fulfil its needs. Durkheim emphasised the role of education in socialising children, teaching them the values and norms of society. Education is part of secondary socialisation teaching children **universalistic standards** i.e. the general standards of society rather than the **particularistic standards** of the family i.e. the specific rules and norms of the family. In other words the school is vital in teaching pupils to fit into wider society and its rules and standards.

So, what are the functions of education?

1. Skills provision– Education teaches children the skills and knowledge they need to be efficient workers and citizens. This includes literacy, numeracy, and all the subjects we learn. What we learn will change as the needs of society change – for example IT has become an important subject because it has become an essential part of work and the economy.

2. Socialisation and Integration– Education helps to socialise children into society by teaching them the necessary values and norms for future work and life in general. So values and norms like hard work, competition, punctuality, obedience etc. are taught, largely through the **Hidden Curriculum**. People must learn to want what society offers – in our society money success, consumer goods etc. They must be **motivated** to succeed. We learn to live in, and have the values and norms necessary for capitalist societies, **(Parsons)**. Through subjects like history and citizenship we learn about our heritage and the values of our society, these help social integration.

3. Stratification and role allocation– The education system allocates people to their position in the Stratification system. In other words education generally decides what level of job you are likely to get. Those who are most able and successful will get the top jobs. This is essential because we need the most able people to do the most important jobs if our economy is to be efficient (that's why such people are paid more!) – **Davis and Moore.**

Young children learning IT skillsl. For Functionalists this shows how the education system has adapted to fit the needs of an economy that is increasingly computer based.

This is why functionalists argue that our education system should be **Meritocratic** i.e. success should be based on ability. Note that education is not just about knowledge and skills. It is about the norms and values needed in society. Pupils must also be motivated to succeed, and want the things – good job, high living standards etc. - that success brings.

How does education fulfil these functions?

Values and norms are not just taught directly. They are part of the **hidden curriculum**, which is part of the **ethos** or **culture** of the school. This is learned in many ways, both inside and outside lessons. :-

1. **Exams** are competitive and individualistic – reflecting the dominant values of society. Pupils learn to be competitive.

2. **Rituals** – assemblies, prefects, prizes etc. teach moral messages, reward hard work and ability.

3. **Authority structures** in schools reflect those of work and outside society.

Evaluation/criticisms

1. Functionalism is **deterministic**. It sees "pupils as the product of school" (as well as family etc. and the other structures of society). They are like sponges who soak up the knowledge, skills values etc. that school gives them. But don't some children rebel? Don't they reject the schools message?

2. Functionalists argue that the education system should be meritocratic – the best students get best jobs – but it isn't. Marxists show how, in reality, class background is as important as intelligence. The system is biased against the working class.

3. Many functionalists argue that I.Q. tests and exams ensure that the most able succeed, but these are culturally biased – they favour white, m/c kids.

4. Marxists argue that Functionalism is "ideological" it justifies and legitimises inequalities - makes the system seem fair.

Test your understanding

1. What are the three major functions of education?

2. Why do functionalists believe that society should be meritocratic.?

3. Discuss and produce examples of the way in which schools, according to functionalists, reinforce accepted values and norms through the hidden curriculum

4. Write a paragraph explaining how education is related to the economy.

Marxism

There are similarities between Marxist and Functionalist perspectives. Both focus on the Educational System and its role in society – **a Structuralist/systems approach**. Both see Education as providing the knowledge, skills, values etc necessary for the economic system and wider society, but **whereas functionalists see this as benefiting society and the individual and reinforcing value consensus, Marxists argue that education helps reproduce the class system and its inequalities**. Marxists see society as being based on class conflict and serving the needs of capitalism and the interests of the Ruling Class. Marxists have an essentially negative view of the 'functions' of education in its present form.

Marxist theory of education

Education produces workers with different levels of skills and abilities to meet the needs of Capitalism. Whereas "higher class" pupils will generally end up with "top jobs" w/c pupils will end up with w/c jobs.

The system is **not therefore meritocratic**. W/c pupils have less chance of success because of the economic and cultural inequalities they suffer.

Education is part of the **I.S.A. (Ideological State Apparatus)**. Education puts across the

> **Ideology** – culture, values, beliefs of the Ruling Class as if it were in the interests of everyone. It as a means of controlling the lower classes, teaching them to be obedient punctual workers.
>
> This is achieved, partly, through the **hidden curriculum**, which puts across the ideology of the Ruling class – emphasising individuality, competition etc., and the other values of capitalism.

> **Key Study – Bowles and Gintis 'Schooling in Capitalist America' (1976)**
>
> **Bowles and Gintis** show how the organisation and hierarchy of the school, its rules and authority structure, reflect the hierarchies of Capitalist industry and society. Pupils are taught to respect authority and to know their place, they are taught to be "good workers" in the future. Schools teach the same values and norms – hard work, competition, punctuality and appropriate dress – qualities that will be needed in the workplace. **External rewards** are emphasised – good grades in school lead to good pay at work. School, like work, is **alienating,** pupils are controlled and have little input into what they learn and how – just like workers have little control over their jobs. This is called **correspondence theory** – because the school corresponds (is similar to) capitalist businesses.

You may have noticed similarities between the Marxist and Functionalist approaches. Both see education as the means by which pupils are prepared for work and adult life in general but whereas Functionalists see this as basically fair and meritocratic, Marxists see it as unfair, as helping to maintain the privileges of the Dominant class and make the lower orders accept their position.

Structuralist Marxist Approaches

Structural Marxists, see **Cultural** factors as being important in explaining how the education system works. They argue that people unconsciously learn culture and automatically carry it on.

> **Bourdieu** argues that schools are responsible for cultural reproduction and this helps reproduce the class system. Schools are basically upper/middle class institutions i.e. Teachers, values and norms are m/c. M/c pupils thus have a big advantage when they go to school. They have been taught the same values, beliefs etc. as the school so they have **cultural capital** whereas w/c pupils have been taught differently and are at a disadvantage - **cultural deficit.** Good examples of cultural capital are the ways in which m/c parents can 'play the system' e.g. use the appeals system to get their kids into the best schools (sometimes even buy an expensive house to get into a good catchment area).

Another classic example comes from **Bernstein.** He argues that m/c children learn a more **elaborate code** of language – more abstract, conceptual and generalised, with a wide vocabulary, whereas w/c children learn a **restricted code,** more concrete and particular. Schools use the elaborate code so w/c pupils are at a disadvantage as they, literally, don't speak the same language as their teachers, they have to learn this. They have a **cultural deficit.**

M/c children learn the value of **deferred gratification**– to be prepared to make sacrifices so that they will benefit in the future, to do homework, stay on at school etc. W/c values tend towards **immediate gratification. Althusser** argues that education, like the media, is part of the **Ideological State Apparatus,** which puts across the interests of the Ruling Class. Pupils are taught to accept their place in society. The **hidden curriculum** helps to prepare w/c children for their future roles as obedient, punctual workers. The whole education system serves the needs of the Capitalist economic system – it produces workers suitable for different positions in the economy. **Basically w/c kids are prepared for w/c jobs.** Middle class language and culture is presented as superior to that of the w/c. W/c kids who want to get on have to learn m/c culture. The exam system helps **legitimate inequalities.** Exams seem fair. Everybody has the same chance. So w/c kids accept their failure and the likelihood that they will end up with lower paid jobs.

Evaluation/criticisms

1. Marxists are criticised for being **deterministic.** They see people as products of the class and educational systems. This ignores the fact that many pupils rebel. Also there are other influences on pupils – home, community etc. so they don't just accept the system, and their position in it.

2. Many w/c pupils do succeed and go on to University and m/c jobs –**social mobility**.

3. Not all teachers accept the system. Many are left wing and critical and question it.

Glenn Rikowski (2005), however argues that Marxist analysis is still important. He points to the fact that schools are now run as 'businesses', competing with each other for pupils; and that some aspects of school provision are now run by private business e.g. school dinners. In addition we might add that the new Academy and Free schools are part financed by private business and that upward social mobility has been **decreasing** for a number of years.

Test your understanding

1. Explain, using examples the process of **cultural reproduction**, including the terms **cultural capital** and **cultural deficit**.

2. Marxists argue that education is **ideological.** Explain what they mean by this. Think about your own schooling. Do you think that any part of it is ideological? Give examples.

3. What are the similarities, and differences, between Marxist and Functionalist views of the **hidden curriculum?**

4. Outline the links Marxists make between education and the economy.

Note that both Functionalist and Marxist sociologists take a structuralist approach: focussing on the relations between the educational system and other institutions, in particularly the economy – a Macro approach. In the next section we will look at an approach that focuses on what happens at the micro level – in the classroom.

Interactionism

Interactionists see society as being based on the everyday interactions of individuals. People have free will and are not just the product of "social structures". They have choices. **Interpretive** Sociologists therefore reject the determinism of other perspectives. Pupils aren't just "passive receivers" who accept what their teachers, and other adults tell them. In order to understand how the system works you need to look at the **micro level** – what happens in the classroom.

The relationships between teacher and pupils and pupils and pupils are crucial as they determine what happens in the classroom i.e. **the social reality of the classroom is negotiated**. Of course it is generally the teacher who has the most power in these negotiations and this is reflected in classroom interaction and rituals – Teachers ask questions, demand answers, control what is learned, students respond, obey etc. But relationships do vary and this is why every classroom is different – in some pupils may mess about, disobey etc. **Labelling** is crucial. Teachers, generally, have the power to categorise pupils as clever/stupid, conscientious/lazy, good/bad etc. and through their treatment of pupils reinforce these labels. Thus pupils often "live up" to these labels – hence a '**self-fulfilling prophecy'** is established.

Hargreaves et al (1975) analysed the way in which the process of labelling works. They used the method of **overt observation** .They found there were three stages :

Speculation – teachers begin to make 'guesses' about their pupils ability and attitude, based on their appearance, enthusiasm , manners etc.

Elaboration – teachers 'test these assumptions (hypotheses) in their everyday interaction with students to see if their prediction is right.

53

Stabilisation –the teachers' labels stick. Their original assumptions are generally confirmed. This is often because the teacher tends to interpret what the pupils do in terms of the label they have given them e.g. if a pupil labelled as 'being of poor ability' does a good piece of homework, the teacher may assume he has copied it.

Think of your own examples of labelling, S.F.P. from your own experience. How accurate do you think Hargreaves analysis is?

Methods link

In **"Pygmalion in the Classroom" (1968) Rosenthal and Jacobson** did a **field experiment** i.e. an experiment done in a pupils natural environment so that the situation is more **ecologically valid i.e. true to lif**e. They decided to test the effects of teachers' attitudes on pupils performance. They told teachers at a school that they were going to give children an intelligence test.

After the children had taken the test the researchers told the teachers they had identified some pupils who were 'spurters' and would improve dramatically over the next year. Sure enough when they returned these pupils had improved much more than the others.

However what the teachers did not know was that so called tests were a sham, and thrown away as soon as they were collected in. The researchers had picked the names of the 'spurters' at random. The reason these children had improved was because of the teachers attitudes. They had, unconsciously, given these pupils more time, support and attention.

Labelling is closely related to **streaming and setting. Cicourel** shows how m/c pupils, because of their values, manners, dress, language (cultural factors) etc. are likely to be put in higher streams than w/c or black students. Then of course **self-fulfilling prophecy** kicks in and pupils in lower streams and sets deteriorate whilst those in higher streams improve. Through these processes schools and teachers define success and failure, but not in any **meritocratic** way.

Though teachers have the most power pupils will also try to impress their peers. This can lead to disruption and conflict if an **anti-school subculture dominates** in the classroom. Most pupils however are neither strongly anti nor pro school. They can go either way, depending on the situation in the classroom.

Evaluation/Criticisms

Interactionists underestimate the importance of outside factors – family, class, culture etc in affecting education.

It is what pupils bring to the classroom that is crucial – this is the basis for labelling.

Labelling theory assumes pupils live up to labels. Labelling may be unfair but:

a)Labels may be accurate

b)Labels are complex not just good or bad – different teachers may label pupils differently – and labels can change.

c)Pupils may reject and react against labels. **Gilbourn and Cripps** showed how West Indian girls in a school worked hard to prove their teacher wrong.

Test your understanding

1. What do Interactionists mean when they say that the "social reality of the classroom is negotiated? (think of your own experience and give examples).

2. Explain how labelling and S.F.P. may affect the performance of pupils.

3. What evidence is there to show that negative labelling does not always cause pupils to fail?

4. What does Rosenthal and Jacobsons experiment show us about the effects of teachers' attitudes on pupils' performance.

54

5. Some sociologists have criticised this experiment on ethical (moral) grounds. Can you think of any ethical criticisms of this experiment?

6. Briefly explain the key differences between the Interactionist approach to education and that of structuralists (Marxists and Functionalists).

The New Right

The **New Right** have dominated educational policy since the 1980s, particularly under the Conservative Governments of 1979 to 1997. The New Right are strong supporters of capitalism. They believe that freedom and economic success are both a product of the 'free market'. The New Right argue that "**market principles**" should be applied to education. Schools should **compete** for pupils and parents should be able to **choose** the best school for their children, with the help of published results. Poor schools would then have to get better or close.

The New Right believe in strict discipline and teacher directed learning. They also see education as essentially training for work and so emphasise **Vocational education**. i.e. education that trains pupils in the skills and values necessary for working life (and the economy).

Evaluation/Criticisms

. The New Right have been criticised for dividing education into education for the elite and training for the rest.

. The market reforms they have established are seen as unfair and unworkable – schools in poor run down areas are bound to get poor results in the League tables.

. New Right theorists such as **Charles Murray** are criticised for arguing that educational inequalities are 'natural' the result of genes rather than society. In particular his view that different 'races' have different levels of ability has been strongly attacked

Note - See, and use, the material in the 'Educational Reforms/Policies' section when answering questions on the New Right. There are full details and exercises on their policies in that section

Feminism

Feminists, like Marxists, are **conflict theorists**, indeed many take a 'Marxist type' approach but instead of focussing on class inequalities in education **they emphasize the inequalities faced by females.** They see society as **Patriarchal – male dominated** and examine the ways education transmits and reproduces gender inequalities.

In the 1970s Feminist studies focussed on the reasons why girls did not do as well as boys in school, and were far less likely to go on to Higher Education. Since this period girls have overtaken boys in many areas of educational performance, however Feminists argue that girls still face a number of obstacles and inequalities in terms of the subjects they do and the way they are treated in schools.

Evaluation/Criticisms

1. The most obvious criticism of Feminist theory is that girls do better than boys in schools these days. The work of Feminist sociologists like **Stanworth and Sue Sharpe** (see Gender and Education) has helped to produce significant changes that have benefited girls in many ways

2. A less obvious criticism is with the Feminist focus on girls. Marxist, and other critics, argue that class is a far more important factor in educational inequalities.

Note - See, and use, the material in the 'Gender and Education' section when answering questions on Feminism/Gender. There are full details of Feminist theory and studies, and exam questions, in that section.

Test your understanding

1. Why do the 'New Right' argue that education should be marketised?

2. Why is it likely that schools in poor w/c areas will do badly in the league tables?

3. What do feminists mean when they say education is patriarchal? How would critics challenge the view that education is patriarchal?

Education and the economy

In a way all the perspectives see education as a preparation for work and adult society, but whereas the New Right and Functionalists emphasise the positive nature of this, Marxists are highly critical. Feminists also argue that education prepares girls for stereotypical, women's jobs.

Since the Conservative government of the 1980s, and the dominance of New Right theory, there has been a big emphasis on **Vocationalism** in education i.e. training in skills directly related to employment. Things like work experience, G.N.V.Q.S, Key Skills etc. The idea being to produce a highly skilled workforce, for an increasingly competitive, global economy.

(See also Education Reforms – Vocationalism.)

Exercise It is essential in sociology to be able to **apply** theories to different areas of study. Take **education and the economy**. If you had to answer a question like:

'Evaluate sociological explanations of the ways in which education contributes to the economic system.'

You would need to look at: **Functionalist, New Right, Marxist and Feminist theories** (less so Interactionism).

You would have to use examples from the **hidden curriculum** and look at **Educational reforms/policie**s and in particular **vocationalism** (which we will look at in more detail later).

Bearing all this in mind produce either a "**brainmap**" or an **A3 summary sheet** that you could use to answer the essay question above.

Inequalities in Education – Differential achievement

Note -The theories we have looked at are all important in explaining inequalities in education. Always use theories in answering questions on inequality.

There are both **inequalities of opportunity** in education i.e. some pupils have less chance than others and **differential achievement** i.e. some pupils attain more in terms of qualifications. Sociologists have found inequalities relating to social class, gender and ethnicity. Some of these inequalities relate to background/home/culture, others relate to the school, but the two areas are closely connected – pupils' backgrounds often affect the way they are treated in school.

Social class and inequalities

Learning Objectives

1. Knowledge and understanding of different explanations of class inequalities in educational achievement.

2. Knowledge, understanding and evaluation of theories and evidence of class inequalities in education.

3. Analysis and evaluation of the role of home and school factors in explaining class inequalities in education. Understanding of how these factors overlap.

4. Analysis and evaluation of the role of cultural and material factors in explaining class inequalities in education

---

We have already mentioned a number of explanations as to why w/c pupils do not do as well as m/c pupils. We should note that it is particularly the "**lower**" **w/c or "underclass" who do very badly** – poverty is a key factor in educational failure. Note also that despite the huge increase in pupils doing A-levels and going on to University the children of Professional people still have a far greater chance of doing so than the w/c (five times better). In 2003 77% of 'professional class' children achieved five GCSE grades at 'C' or above compared with only 32% of the children of **manual workers.**

Explanations of class inequalities in education

Natural/genetic

Charles Murray (The Bell Curve), a **New Right** sociologist, argues that w/c, blacks etc. are less intelligent i.e. have lower IQs as measured by tests. This is rejected by most Sociologists who criticise the cultural bias of IQ tests and point to environmental factors as the key to achievement. I.Q. tests are made and set by white m/c people mostly males, it is therefore not surprising that white m/c pupils do best at them. One IQ test question asked pupils to work out a series of anagrams – ZOMART, RHAMBS etc, these of course are classical composers, but you would be much more likely to know that if you were m/c! This is cultural knowledge not intelligence. **Labov** gave w/c, black kids tests outside the formal setting of the classroom, and found they did much better in more natural, comfortable surroundings. Moreover even if we accept IQ (etc.) test results w/c kids of the same, measured, ability do less well than m/c kids.

Home factors

1. Family - Lower w/c families are likely to be bigger and there are far more single parent families. Children from such families are likely to do worse because of **cultural and material deprivation**. Single parents families are often poor, and have no male role model. Children from such families are more likely to get into trouble, truant and get suspended or expelled. Again the **New Right** point to the large number of unmarried mothers in the underclass who do not provide the support their children need

2. Material deprivation – Poor diet, housing, low living standards lead to illness and absence from school. Lack of money may mean no private place to study, lack of books and other educational toys and resources. Many very poor w/c families live in bed and breakfast accommodation, even more have to share bedrooms. All of these factors can lead to failure.

Research study (Lisa Harker 2006)

Harker produced a report for the Housing Charity Shelter, in which she reviewed a range of available evidence i.e. she used Secondary Sources –studies made by other researchers. She identifies a number of negative effects that poverty may have on children's educational performance:

1. **Less room to play** leads to slower cognitive development, more mental illness (especially depression) and aggressive behaviour.

2. **Less space for study** and poor conditions for homework – noisy, cramped overcrowded.

3. Many poor families tend to **move house** a lot thus causing disruption to schooling.

4. **Hazards to health** - damp housing, poorer diet and more accidents in the home – leading to absence from school.

5. **Higher rates of divorce, separation and mental illness amongst parents** – thus meaning they are less supportive.

Methods link: Harker used Secondary sources in her research. Such an approach saves both time and money as in this case such sources are readily available. It would also have enabled her to produce a far more wide-ranging report than she would have been able to using primary research. She could also have compared research to test its reliability (reliability in sociology refers to whether research can be repeated and produce 'the same' results). In this case Harker would have been examining whether the research she looked at gave similar results.

> **There are however problems in using secondary sources:**
>
> Because you haven't done the research yourself you don't have any control over the methods used, so it hard to say how valid (accurate/true to life) it is.
>
> Similarly there may also be bias. Researchers may have been committed to the idea of educational equality and perhaps 'found what they were looking for'.
>
> Harker herself was working for Shelter, a charity for the homeless, therefore she might well have tended to be selective i.e. using the material which backed the views of the charity.

Many people are surprised when sociologists claim that poverty is a major cause of educational failure. They think that poverty is rare in modern Britain. Certainly **Absolute Poverty** –lacking basics such as food clothing and shelter is less of a problem than in the past but **Relative Poverty**, where people are poor compared with the accepted standards of society, is still common. This leads t o **marginalisation,** where poor pupils feel excluded, because they do not have the clothes, holidays, computers and other 'stuff' that more affluent pupils take for granted. This of course can lead to truancy, bullying, low self esteem and even mental illness and aggression.

The Labour Government made the elimination of childhood poverty a key policy, after it was elected in 1997, but although early results were promising the figure started to go up again in 2006. The Government's own figures show that 2.4 million children were living in poverty in 2008 and this number has increased subsequently.

3. Cultural factors - most sociologists consider cultural factors to be crucial. **Cultural deprivation** - in his 1960s-70s classic **longitudinal study Douglas** argues that many working class pupils lack the support and stimulation necessary to succeed. There is lack of parental support and help at home and w/c parents are less likely to visit schools, and talk to the head-teacher.

There is a **lack of books and other educational stimulus** – visits to museums, holidays etc. Children are also likely to be encouraged to go to work to contribute to family income and are more likely to truant; often to help out at home or because of the value of immediate gratification - they think school is boring, a waste of time and want to have fun now. Some functionalist sociologists argue that w/c children seek **immediate gratification** they want to have fun now whilst m/c pupils learn the value of **deferred gratification** i.e. they are prepared to forgo immediate pleasure because they know that by working hard at school they will be better off in the future. **New Right** sociologists such as **Charles Murray (1990s)** have updated this approach. They argue that at the 'bottom of society' there is an **underclass** whose values are different from the rest of society. They are often benefit dependent and have a 'something for nothing' attitude, they are also 'anti-authority'. They see no value in education and pass these values on to their children.

Note the **connection between cultural and material deprivation**. Parents may not be able to afford books, computers etc (material deprivation), or they may not value education and not see them as a priority (cultural deprivation).

Home and School factors - links

Cultural reproduction is a Marxist concept. Marxists argue that the school is a m/c institution and w/c pupils are at a disadvantage because they have a **cultural deficit**. **Bernstein** argues that w/c pupils literally speak a different language. It is not that w/c culture is inferior just different. (**w/c** pupils have a **restricted code** that is context bound and has a limited vocabulary compared with m/c **elaborate code** – more complex and generalised language –**see also Marxist theory**)

Ball (1994) shows how m/c parents are able to use their '**cultural capital**' to work the system and make sure their children go to the "best" schools – they use the appeals system, impress the head, and even move house to get into catchment areas with good schools.

Paul Willis, Learning to Labour (1976). In a classic application of this theory, Willis studied **cultural reproduction** in a boy's Secondary School. He found a strong conflict between the "Lads" (w/c, anti-school subculture) and the "lobes" (hard working pro-school pupils). The lads saw school as an alien and pointless institution. They knew they would not succeed so, in order to gain status, they turned the norms and values of the school "upside down". Hard work, politeness etc. became "bad", messing around, cheeking teachers, being late, smoking etc. became good. **The lads did not value qualifications** but street wisdom (banter and quick wit).Willis argues that this shows "cultural reproduction". The lads are, unconsciously, preparing themselves for their future, boring, manual, jobs. They are learning to "get by" and so their "rebellion" is actually functional for the system.

Methods link Willis adopted an **"eclectic"** approach combining a Marxist view with Interpretive methods. He studied only one school and about a dozen 'lads'. This is therefore an example of a **case study**. Case studies often involve a variety of methods. Willis used overt observation, so the pupils knew he was studying them. This has many advantages: it means that the observer is being ethical, because he has the consent of the subjects of his research. It also means that he can ask questions (Willis also used unstructured interviews). Such interpretive methods allow the researcher to establish a bond with those they are studying and to uncover their '**motives and meanings'**. Because of this closeness the researcher can **empathise** – see the world through their subject's eyes, and this tends to produce **valid (true to life) results**. Positivist critics however would argue that such a small sample **cannot give representative results**, and that it is **not objective.** They would also argue that it is **not reliable** as it would be very unlikely that anyone repeating the research would get the same results. The 'lads' may have also 'played up' to Willis and thus not behaved naturally – **the Hawthorne Effect** – for a fuller discussion see the 'Methods' section of this book.

School factors

Processes within the school also contribute to class inequalities:

Peer group pressure – Because of the alienation, failure and labelling they experience w/c pupils are far more likely to develop '**Anti-school subcultures'** – (**see Willis above, and Subculture section, below).**

Streaming, Labelling and Self –fulfilling Prophecy – **Interactionists** emphasise the way in which working class (etc.) pupils are more likely to be put in **lower streams** and subject to **negative labelling** which affects their progress (**see Interactionist theories page 10**)

Much research has focussed on the effects of background on educational performance, however **Rutter (1979)** – in his study of 12 Inner London Schools found that schools do make a big difference. He found that some schools do better than others irrespective of class, ethnicity etc. Schools with **strong leadership from the head, a positive ethos, consistent discipline, clear aims and values** and **good teaching** got better results. A **School Inspectors report** into thirty '**Failing Schools' (2008)** supported these conclusions.

This study has been used by Governments to "put the blame on schools" for educational failure. However Rutter's study was not representative and was only limited. He also never claimed that "home/class" factors were not important.

Test your understanding

1. How might poverty affect the performance of children in school?

2. In what ways may some children be culturally deprived?

3. In what ways can the school 'reproduce class inequalities'?

4. Explain the connections between home and school factors.

Ethnic inequalities in education

Learning objectives

1. Knowledge and understanding of different explanations of ethnic inequalities in education.
2. Knowledge, understanding and evaluation of theories and evidence of ethnic inequalities in education.
3. Analysis and evaluation of the role of home and school factors in explaining ethnic inequalities in education. Understanding of how these factors overlap.
4. Analysis and evaluation of the role of cultural and material factors in explaining ethnic inequalities in education

The nature of ethnic inequalities in education is complicated. Some ethnic groups do as well as or even better than whites e.g. Indians and Chinese pupils. Others do worse – West Indians, Pakistanis and some Bangladeshis. The issue is further complicated by the effects of class and gender: those groups who do well tend to be more m/c, whilst some ethnic minorities place less value on education for girls. Again there are a number of explanations for inequalities:

Genetic explanations

The **New Right**, some **Psychologists** and some **Functionalists** argue that black students have lower intelligence than whites and Asians. **Charles Murray (The Bell curve)** a New Right sociologist, argues that IQ tests show that blacks are less able. Most sociologists reject this. As we have seen IQ tests are culturally biased. Labov showed that black children scored higher results when taken out of the classroom and interviewed in a less intimidating atmosphere, and a less formal way – **an advantage of unstructured interviews.**

Home factors

1. Material Deprivation – Ethnic groups that do badly are predominantly working class and suffer in the same way as the white lower classes – poor diets and housing, absence from school, lack of educational toys, books, computers etc. The **Swann Report** concluded that 50% of black under achievement was due to class factors. The Joseph Rowntree Foundation (2007) estimated that up to 70% of Bangladeshi and 50% of Pakistani children grow up in poverty (compared to 20% of whites). But this cannot be the only factor, Indian children have similar levels of poverty to black West Indians yet do far better in education, and White British pupils who are poor do worse than any other group.

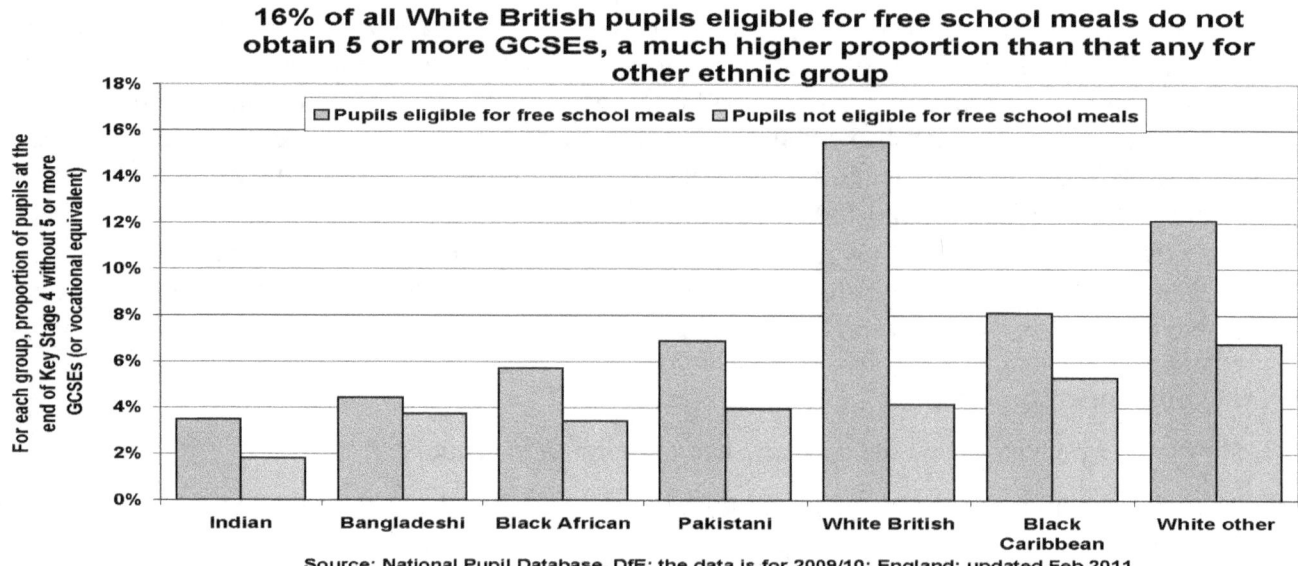

Source: National Pupil Database, DfE; the data is for 2009/10; England; updated Feb 2011

2. Cultural factors – Functionalists see lack of integration as being crucial – recent studies show big improvements for some minorities, for example Bengalese, who have become increasingly integrated into British society. In fact Bangladeshi students (the most recent large immigrant, Asian group) have made the most significant gains at GCSE level. In 1992 only 14% of Bangladeshi children achieved 5 GCSE passes at 'C' grade or above now the figure is 57%, as high as whites.

Driver and Ballard (1979) found that some Asian children (e.g. **Indians and Chinese**) do well because the close knit extended families they belong to are strongly supportive of education whereas West Indian families are often poor, single parent and anti-school. However **Tony Sewell (1997)** found that most West Indian families had high aspirations for their children's education, but the fact that such families were often **single parent** and **matriarchal** meant that boys lacked role models/discipline and self esteem. They can often be drawn into anti-school gangs with aggressive masculine values, and become disruptive in lessons – challenging teachers' authority. In contrast West Indian girls have largely "caught up" with whites, showing that they value education, this can be put down to the same factor – the matriarchal nature of their families which gives them **higher status and self esteem** (though some may be anti-school).

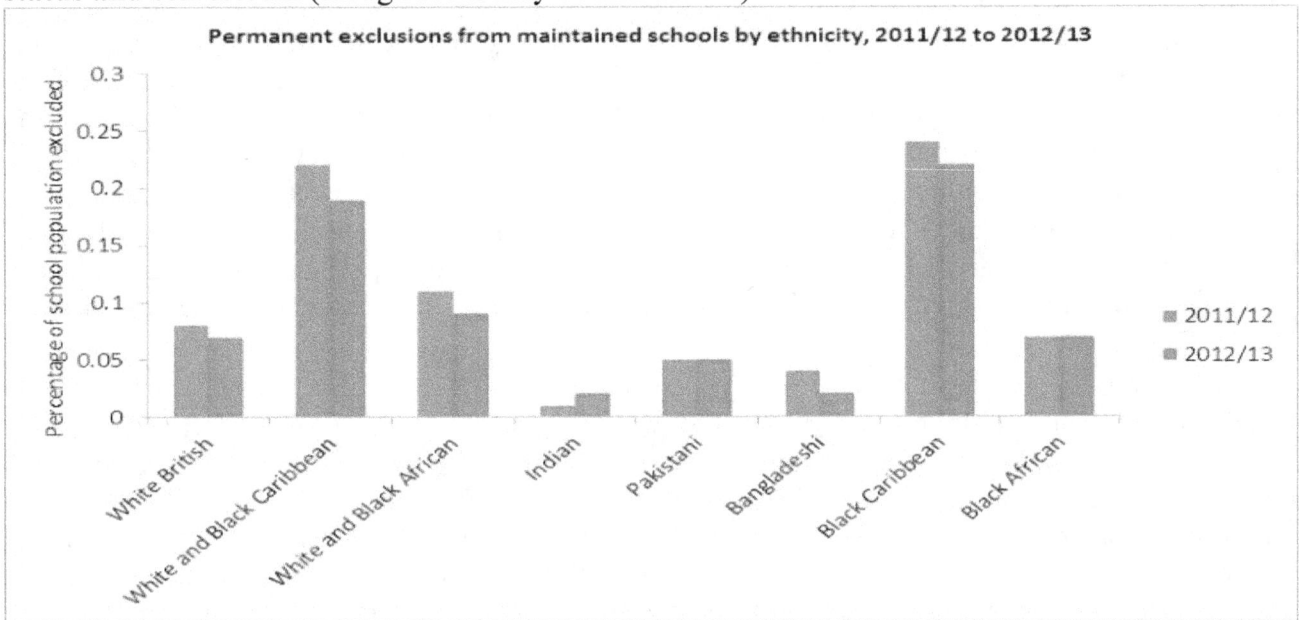

Source: Adapted from O.N.S.

Another factor is that some Asians (mostly Pakistanis and Bangladeshis) may send their children back to their country of origin at crucial periods of their education – thus causing disruption. **New Right** sociologists argue that this 'lack of willingness' to integrate is a key factor in educational failure.

Language is also important. For some Asian groups, for example **Pakistanis**, English is an **additional language,** and this may hold back their educational progress. However Indian, and now Bangladeshi children, have proved that this is not necessarily a barrier to performance. Indian children do better than whites in GCSEs, and Bangladeshis now do as well.

West Indians often speak with a strong dialect (Creole) this again holds them back, as it does not fit in with the (m/c) language code used in schools. The development of a "rap culture" with its' own slang has given cause for concern. This culture is anti-school and often violent in its language. It has become an important part of many Black Anti-school subcultures.

School factors

Ethnic minorities may suffer racism – both direct and indirect. Text books often show negative images of blacks – starvation, slavery etc and this may be communicated in lessons, lowering the self esteem and confidence of ethnic minority pupils. Most of the potential role models they may learn about in history and other subjects are white. **Joseph Gevarughese (1987)** argues that the contributions of non-whites to the development of maths, science, philosophy etc. are all but ignored in the school curriculum, which is resolutely European progressing from the Ancient Greeks to the Renaissance to modern Europe. The major contributions of Ancient civilizations like Mesopotamia India and Persia, as well as China and the Arabs are barely mentioned.

The **Hidden Curriculum** is white as well as middle class, there is **Cultural Reproduction** of racism as well as class inequality. The vast majority of teachers are white and therefore children from ethnic minorities do not have many, successful '**ethnic role models'.** However the fact that some minorities do very well in the system means that this, again, cannot be the sole reason for inequalities.

Teachers, classroom organisation and labelling – key studies

---

1. Cecille Wright (1986- 1992), used **observation** to study racism in both Primary and Secondary schools. She found that West Indian children are often labelled by teachers as disruptive and badly behaved. They were far more likely to be put in low streams and sets even when their ability matched that of white and Asian pupils in higher sets. The result was that S.F.P. set in and black pupils tended to give up and rebel. West Indian children are also 4 times as likely to be excluded from school.

2. David Gilbourns's research (1990) again using ethnographic techniques - observation and interviews with teachers and pupils - supports Wright. He found that although the vast majority of teachers try to treat all children fairly many had ethnocentric views regarding West Indian students as "trouble" so more were likely to be disciplined, reported and excluded than other pupils who committed similar offences.

3. Smith and Tomlinson, however, found that class was more important than race in explaining the underachievement of ethnic minorities. They found little evidence of racism in the results of the **Questionnaires** that they used. Ethnicity had little effect on performance, the school was much more important.

Methods link

Both Wright and Gilbourn used **ethnographic approaches**, favoured by **Interactionist Sociologists,** by immersing themselves in the culture of the schools that they studied in order to achieve a more **valid (**true to life) picture. By actually observing the treatment of ethnic minorities you are less likely to be deceived. Ethnographic approaches are also more **empathetic** , because the researcher is involved in the day to day culture of the school, they get to understand the meanings and feelings of the people concerned – both teachers and pupils. Though the subjects may 'put on an act' at first, if observed in an **overt (open) way** it is likely that in time they will behave normally, these methods achieve far grater **depth and detail**. Probing questions may be asked to clarify and deepen knowledge.

However the presence of the researcher may cause unnatural behaviour (**the Hawthorne effect).** Teachers may**,** for example try to hide racist attitudes. Such methods are also very dependent on the **interpretations** of the researcher. Other researchers may see the situation in a very different way. Thus these methods are **unreliable** (if repeated it is unlikely that they would get **the same results).** The small number of schools involved in both studies cannot possibly be seen as **representative** of the thousands of schools in Britain, therefore we cannot **generalise** these results.

Smith and Tomlinson took a more **Positivist** approach. They used **questionnaires. These would provide** a much more **representative** approach, as they could, potentially be sent to thousands of students and teachers over a wide area. They would also probably be more **reliable**, if the sample used was **representative.** However a topic like racism is likely to produce **invalid** responses. It is a sensitive subject and teachers may not wish to appear racist. Therefore they may give **socially acceptable** answers. Furthermore if **closed questions** are used the researcher cannot probe for deeper meanings and reasons.

The role of the **Hidden Curriculum** is again crucial here. The racism of society is reproduced through education –**cultural reproduction**- and other influences , family, media stereotyping etc.

Test your understanding

1) Ethnic inequalities in education are more about class than ethnicity. Explain this statement.

2) Examine the ways in which cultural factors affect the educational achievement of ethnic minorities.

3. Outline the effects of the hidden curriculum on the achievement of ethnic minorities. (including school organisation – labelling streaming etc).

Gender inequalities

Learning Objectives

1. Understanding the relationship between gender and educational achievement.

2. Knowledge and understanding of changes in the educational achievement of boys and girls and the reasons for these changes.

3. Knowledge, understanding and analysis of different theories and studies of gender inequalities in education.

Gender inequalities are complex. In recent years girls have significantly improved their GCSE and A-level results, which are now better than boys. They have taken over boys as regards University places but are still far more likely to do humanities and arts subjects whist boys dominate science, engineering, maths etc.

Feminists focus on the **Patriarchal** nature of schools and society in general. They argue that despite the improvement in girl's educational performance they still suffer from many inequalities in education (and when they subsequently enter the workplace).

When examining gender inequalities, we need to focus on three key issues:

1. The inequalities girls have suffered and still suffer.

2. The reasons for the improvement in girls performance.

3. The reasons boys have not improved as much as girls.

This brings us to a key point: **Remember it is not that boys achievements in education have declined, it is that girls have improved their performance much more than boys, in recent years**. Nor is it a simple issue of gender. Class and ethnicity both play a major role.

Explanations of inequalities girls have suffered and still face.

1. Natural/genetic - New Right/Functionalists/ Psychologists – **Tests reveal that girls do better in verbal testing, boys in non-verbal**. This could partly explain differences in female and male achievements – and in particular why girls do better in humanities subjects and languages. Though differences may be the result of socialisation rather than genes. In addition the same theorists **stress the more expressive nature of females – more focussed on feelings, caring and people**. Again this may explain the preferences of girls for humanities rather than science subjects, when they are able to choose their subjects at A-Level and University.

2. Socialisation – Education builds on what we have already learned. Gender differences are the product of family, peer and media influence as well as education. Traditional roles – male provider, female carer/domestic – are reinforced in many ways. **Sue Sharpe** in a study of w/c London girls in the **1970s** found that family and marriage was their priority (but see her later study below). Girls who do 'boys' subjects may also face ridicule from their peers. The media and advertising etc reinforce sexism; parents encourage different qualities in sons and daughters – in short we live in a **Patriarchal society.**

3.A number of studies by feminist sociologists in the 1970s and 1980s demonstrated this '**sexism' in education. Stanworth** (1983) researched A-level students in an F.E. College and found that teachers knew far more boys' names than girls, gave boys more attention and underestimated girls' abilities. Both teachers and students overestimated boys' abilities. **Spender (The invisible women**

1983) found boys received more time from teachers and got away with more – bad behaviour by boys was tolerated. In an experiment she found that work received a higher mark from teachers when they were told it was by a boy!

> **Cultural reproduction** – Just as schools reproduce class inequalities, so they reproduce Patriarchy (**Mitchell**). This is primarily done through the **hidden curriculum** - the values, norms etc. learned indirectly through the ethos and organisation of schools:
>
> . Most Senior Teachers are men. So girls see males as authority figures in everyday school life.
>
> . Girls may be pressured into traditional subjects – arts, humanities - by teachers, peers and parents.
>
> . Reading schemes and books were often sexist e.g. Physics textbooks predominantly show boys doing experiments. Children's reading and storybooks often depict boys as heroes, princes etc. and girls as 'damsels in distress', vulnerable and passive.
>
> . School uniform restricts girls' activities.
>
> . In PE games are often segregated
>
> . Teachers expectations are different – labelling, stereotyping etc.

Of course much has happened since these studies, yet the Hidden Curriculum remains, in many ways, patriarchal and some **feminists** have argued that boys and girls should be taught separately to allow girls more time and attention and stop them being "disrupted" by badly behaved boys. Contemporary evidence shows that whilst sexism in terms of uniform and textbooks has improved considerably, male dominance of senior teaching positions remains. Similarly boys still receive more attention in class (though much of this is negative).

Changing inequalities Female improvements

Over the past 15-20 years girls have greatly improved their educational attainment at all levels. Boys improvement has been far less dramatic. There are a number of explanations for this:

1. Changing attitudes - Feminism and the Women's movement have changed the way girls think about their lives. Careers have become much more important. Remember the **Sue Sharpe** study we looked at earlier? When Sharpe repeated her study in 1994 w/c girls placed much more emphasis on a career, rather than marriage and family, and took equal rights for granted.

2. Role Models. There are now more women in high profile, "top jobs". Britain has had a female Prime Minister (Mrs Thatcher) and businesswomen like Anita Roddick (Body Shop) have shown that women can get to the top in business (though she remains the exception rather than the rule). Perhaps, however, the most important role model that girls have today is their mother! Girls are used to having a mum that works, who has a career, and mothers are far more likely to encourage their daughters into following in their footsteps.

Public Domain Image
Girls are now far more likely to take Science and Technology subjects.

3. Legal changes. The Sex Discrimination Act (1979) and the National Curriculum (1998) mean that it is illegal to 'channel' boys and girls into traditional boys and girls subjects. The National curriculum made it compulsory for all pupils to do sciences and this has produced a big increase in the number of girls taking and passing subjects like GCSE Physics.

4. Work changes The increase in non-manual 'female' jobs – retail, offices, the professions etc. means more employment opportunities for women. At the same time youth unemployment and the decline in "male" traditional w/c jobs has produced uncertainty in young males and may have depressed educational achievement.

5.Changes in marriage and the family The decline in family stability – increases in divorce cohabitation and one-parent families - may have influenced girl's attitudes. Women want to be more financially independent. Increased cohabitation and later marriage are also important in this context.

We should note, however, the fact that class is still a far more important factor in inequality than gender. **Educational improvement amongst both girls and boys is most limited amongst the lowest 20% in the class system**. Girls in this group are far more likely to become pregnant and to remain unqualified. Similarly education for girls is less valued amongst some ethnic groups – though West Indian girls do much better than West Indian boys in education, recognising its importance (and possibly reflecting the matriarchal nature of West Indian families).

Moreover boys are still far more likely to aspire to "top jobs" and do 'higher status' subjects – Science, Technology, Maths etc.

Male underachievement in education

There is currently much concern about the "failure" of boys in education. The first point to note is that boys achievements have **improved not deteriorated** but they have not improved as much as girls.

Explanations for the 'underachievement' of boys include:

. **Teachers attitudes** – teachers are more tolerant of poor behaviour and disruption by boys – they allow boys to "get away with it" and have lower expectations of boy's work. This leads to boys overestimating their ability (girls underestimate theirs!) and not working hard enough for success.

Methods link

A study by **Myhill and Jones (2006)** used **semi-structured interviews** to find out the views of pupils, ranging from years 1-10. They found that an overwhelming majority of pupils thought that teachers treated boys more negatively, in terms of punishments, criticism and even the tone of voice they used. Note however that the sample size for this research was small (144) so could not claim to be representative – though the fact that so many pupils did feel that boys were 'discriminated' against means that it is likely that the results were valid. Semi-structured interviews are extremely useful in this kind of research because they enable the sociologist to get both quantitative, statistical data (what percentage of pupils think boys are treated unfairly) and qualitative data (the reasons for these beliefs and the meanings pupils attach to teacher pupil interactions). However there is the danger (as with all interviews of **interviewer bias**. Did the pupils give the interviewers the answers that they thought they expected – if so the influence of **demand characteristics may lessen the validity of the research.**

. **The Feminisation of education – Melanie Phillips (2002)** argues that there is more emphasis today on 'girl skills' – discussion, creativity etc and less on authority, exams and competition. Education has become 'touchy-feely' and boys find this harder to relate too. Educational success is considered 'girlie', failure masculine. This helps lead to the formation of anti-school subcultures amongst boys and the bullying of boys who do conform - 'geeks'. Boys may achieve status through challenging authority and adopting a macho attitude (see Willis). Critics of Phillips, however, argue that the current educational system is in fact more competitive and has more exams than ever before, so this should favour boys!

3. Socialisation – boys tend to less well-organized, more untidy and less conformist. Girls may well have benefited from the introduction of coursework because they are better organised and plan and present work more effectively. In addition New Right sociologists such as Charles Murray, argue that the increase in female-headed, single parent families mean that many boys have no strong male role model in the family. This can lead to lack of discipline and educational failure etc, this is particularly true for West Indian males who are far more likely to be excluded from school and achieve poor qualifications. Additionally, in Primary Schools, the vast majority of teachers are female – so there are few 'male role models' for young boys.

4. The decline of traditional manual jobs – factory/manufacturing etc., along with the growth of feminism and female opportunities, has led to a "crisis of masculinity" amongst males, particularly w/c males **(Mac an Ghaill 1994)**. Men no longer have a clear provider/breadwinner role and may find it difficult to find 'men's jobs'. This may affect their motivation in school.

Methods link

The research company **Kirkland Rowell (2007)** conducted a **survey** to find out the attitudes of parents towards their children's education. The survey was in the form of a **Questionnaire**. It was sent to 500 secondary schools throughout Britain and was completed by 137,000 students and 280,000 parents – a huge, and representative, sample. Amongst its findings were that 67% of parents with daughters wanted them to go to university, compared to 62% of parents with sons. In addition 80% of girls wanted to go to university compared with 72% of boys. Whilst these differences may not be huge but they are of great significance in showing a fundamental change in attitudes from even 20 or 30 years ago, when it was considered far more important for sons to get qualifications.

This study illustrates some of the **advantages of using questionnaires in national, educational research**. There are millions of people involved in education, all over the country – parents pupils and teachers. To achieve **representative** results (and so that you can **compare** the responses of different regions, and make **generalisations)** you need a method that can reach a large, dispersed, population. Questionnaires such as this produce **quantitative data** and, even when done on this scale, can be quickly analysed using computer technology. We can produce clear, numerical results (as above) and is likely to be **reliable** i.e. if repeated very similar results are likely to be achieved.

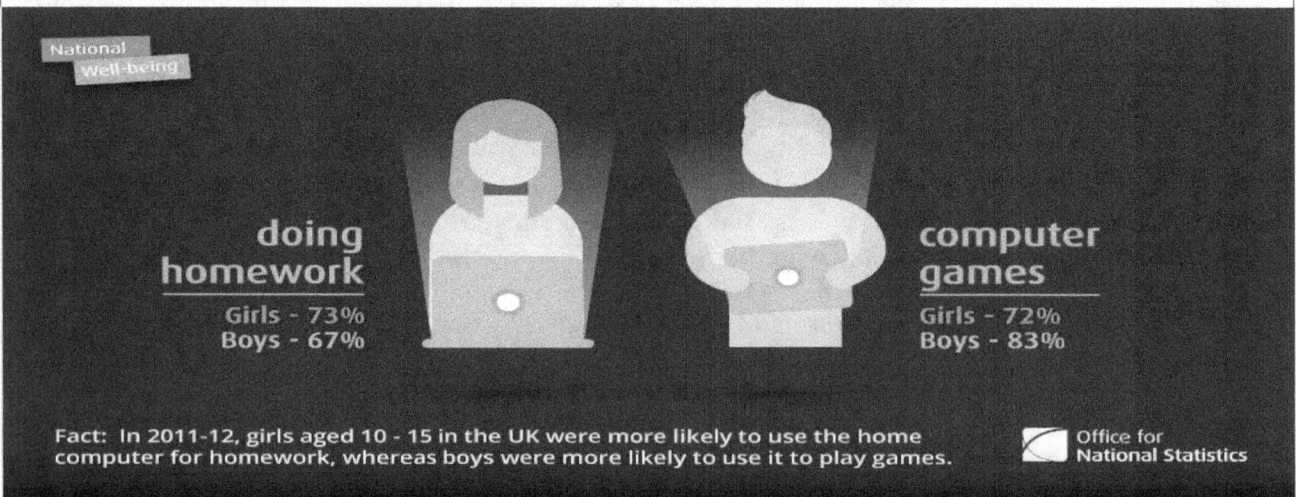

However the major weakness of this method is that the closed questions that must be used to get such statistical data mean that people are unable to expand their answers and show the meanings they attach to them – the reasons behind their responses - they **thus lack depth and detail** and, because respondents may have to 'choose a box to tick' means that they may be forced into an answer that is close but not exactly true. Results can therefore **lack validity**.

Boys and Girls different attitudes and behaviour Source ONS

A note on the Hidden Curriculum – Boys and Girls 'Changing Attitudes'.

You will have noticed that the **Hidden Curriculum** plays a major role in explaining all types of educational inequality. The Curriculum of a school directly teaches the knowledge, values and skills necessary for society e.g. as society becomes more technological etc education becomes more vocational – because of the need for a more technically skilled workforce.
The Hidden Curriculum is, as we have seen, the teaching of a "culture" – norms. values etc, indirectly through the structure and rituals of the school.

Functionalists argue this is essential to our economic and social welfare and stability – we need a disciplined, punctual, law abiding population. Thus school rules, assemblies, prefect systems etc prepare us for future roles. We learn to work hard, compete etc etc.
Marxists agree that such norms and values are taught but they argue that this is to produce a punctual and obedient workforce for capitalism. Critics argue that as well as reproducing the class system, **the Hidden Curriculum also reproduces Patriarchy and Racism – Cultural Reproduction.** When examining all inequalities be aware of the role of the Hidden Curriculum.

Test your knowledge and understanding

1. Produce a comparison chart (two columns) one of which outlines the reasons for the improvement of girls performance in education and the other explaining why boys have failed to improve as much. Draw arrows to link factors in the two columns.

2. Examine the relationship between gender, class and ethnicity in explaining differential educational achievement.

3. In what ways are girls still 'unequal' in terms of education?

Subcultures

Learning objectives
1. Knowledge and understanding of the relationship between membership of 'subcultures' and educational performance.
2. Analysis and evaluation of relevant theories and studies of the effects of subcultures on educational achievement.
3. Understanding of the relationship between subcultures and social background – gender, ethnicity and class.

As we have already seen membership of subcultures has significant effects on educational performance. Subcultures are the product of both social background and experiences at school. **Paul Willis** produced the classic analysis of an anti-school subculture, when he showed how w/c lads in lower streams react by rebelling against the culture of the school and inverting its values. They took a pride in disobedience, messing around, doing the minimum of work, cheeking the teachers etc. This allowed the "macho lads" to gain status from their 'mates'.
There is still a great deal of evidence to support Willis conclusions but things have changed since his study in the late 1970s. Society has become more multi-cultural, girls have dramatically improved their performance and few of the manual jobs 'the lads' would have gone into in factories, mines and other industries, are still available.
Sociologists have therefore concluded that the situation is far more complex than just having "Anti" and "Pro" school subcultures. **Keddie** argues that most pupils are neither for or against the school, and that how they react will depend on the teacher, the lesson, and the proportion of positive and negative pupils in the class. If the "antis" dominate, other pupils will tend to follow them.
Mac an Ghail (1994) identified two other w/c male reactions to school. Many boys, from mostly skilled w/c homes, want to achieve academic success and improve their job prospects. However

they had to adopt ways of coping with the bullying and accusations of effeminacy they got from the 'anti-school lads'. They did this by either putting up with the jokes at their expense or confusing the lads e.g. by deliberately acting in a feminine way. Others '**the new enterprisers**' rejected the traditional academic curriculum but took advantage of the new '**Vocational**' courses that became available in the 1980s, GNVQs etc, and succeeded in subjects like business studies and computing.

Mac an Ghail also identified a group of m/c boys from professional backgrounds who also rejected what their teachers had to offer, seeing their own culture and knowledge as superior. They despised both the 'academic achievers' and 'new enterprisers'. They did however aspire to University and a professional job and therefore would work hard enough to succeed without appearing to do so.

O'Donnel (1991) showed how different ethnic groups responded differently to education and to the racism they sometimes experienced. **West Indian boys** often reacted angrily to the white dominated educational system, and hence had high levels of exclusion, whereas **Indian boys** may also feel angry but do not reject education, instead they try to use the system for their own benefit. Of course home and family background have a big effect here (**see ethnicity and education**). West Indian girls, again probably influenced by the matriarchal (female dominated) households they come from, also get angry at the patronising attitudes and negative labelling they get from some teachers. However they tend to react by working hard to succeed and prove their teachers wrong (**Gilbourn and Cripps**), at the same time they would also show their rejection of the school culture in their dress, make-up and attitudes in school (**Mizra**).

The study of female subcultures has been limited, it seems girls are generally regarded as being more passive and pro school. Mac an Ghail showed that **female w/c students** often suffered inequality in the new 'Vocational education', taking lower status courses like health and beauty, whilst the boys were doing computing and business. The most recent studies show a class divide between girls. 'Can do girls' from the m/c and higher w/c are mostly pro-school and wish to succeed in education and establish a successful career, however many girls from the lower w/c are adopting ant-school subcultures, and are behaving in more aggressive and defiant ways. In many ways these are the female equivalents of the lads.

Carol Jackson (Lads and Ladettes in school 2006)

Jackson's research in some ways builds on previous ideas but also adds a new dimension. She found that 'laddish behaviour' increasingly applies to female as well as male students; and even to some m/c girls. Swearing, smoking, drinking and misbehaving in school made these girls (and boys) feel 'cool and popular'. Such girls may also resort to excessive femininity – an obsession with make-up and fashion – both of which are discouraged by schools. There is a great fear of being seen as a 'swot' or 'geek'. Jackson argues that there is now so much pressure on pupils to succeed that there is a fear of failure – and of being seen as stupid. Being 'laddish' gets around this perfectly - because you pretend that you haven't worked and don't expect to do well, and if you succeed you're seen as a genius. This is of course what distinguishes some of these, mostly middle class, pupils from the 'lads' in schools who know they are going to fail.

Methods link - Jackson used **semi-structured interviews** in her research on 209 pupils in nine schools, a small unrepresentative sample, but it enabled Jackson to produce both quantitative and qualitative results and, by allowing pupils to **answer some questions 'in depth' and in their own words**, means that results were likely to be **valid**. However Jackson herself had some misgivings about whether she was asking '**leading questions**' and whether pupils were giving her the answers **they thought she wanted**. In addition when questioning pupils of this age it is more than likely that some will answer in a way so as to 'seem cool' in front of the interviewer. Few 14 year-olds want to be seen as geeks!

Test your knowledge and understanding

Draw a brain map showing the different educational subcultures found in schools. For each one briefly describe the attitude of members towards school and the effects on their performance of membership of the subculture and identify the gender, class and ethnicity of the members.

Educational changes and reforms (policies)

Learning objectives

1. Knowledge and understanding of government policies and reforms of education since 1945
2. Knowledge, understanding and analysis of the ideas and ideologies behind reforms – theory links.
3. Analysis and evaluation of the effectiveness of reforms in improving standards and increasing meritocracy.

To understand changes in education you have to understand the concerns of the Government (and the general public) at particular times.

During WW2 the government was appalled by the low standards of education that many ordinary soldiers showed in tests. They therefore introduced the **Butler Act (1944)** which was intended to give a good education to everyone **based on academic ability not ability to pay**. However the **Tripartite system** that was established was heavily criticised by sociologists who discovered that it was very unfair on w/c children. The **Labour Government of 1964** therefore introduced the **Comprehensive** system and **Compensatory education**. The overall aim was to establish **Meritocracy** – achievement based on ability (which **Functionalists** argued was essential to ensure that the "brightest people did the top jobs"). This would ensure an efficient economy and everyone would be better off.

We can divide educational reforms/policies into three periods (plus, current Coalition/Conservative policies):

Educational policies - 1945 - 1970s

This was influenced by **Social democrat/Liberal/ Functionalist ideas** - the ideal of **Meritocracy.** There was a broad range of agreement amongst the political parties. There was a concern that the system was not fair and that much **w/c talent was wasted**.

The Butler act (1944) – set up the **Tripartite system – Grammar Schools, Technical Schools and Secondary Moderns** – this was supposed to give children the right education to match their abilities: Grammars for the academic, Technicals for the more technically minded, Secondary Moderns for the rest. **Selection** was based on **11+ intelligence tests,** i.e. the system was **selective.**

> **Criticisms of the system (Douglas, Jackson, Halsey etc)**
>
> . **11+/I.Q. tests are culturally biased**, discriminating against w/c, ethnic minorities and late developers
>
> . Children were **labelled** as failures at the age of 11. Many gave up and underachieved (SFP).
>
> 3. **Secondary Modern Schools had low status** and pupils took lower level exams (C.S.E.s)
>
> 4. The system was **socially divisive**. Grammar schools were mostly m/c. The w/c were less likely to go to Grammar Schools irrespective of ability
>
> 5. There were **not enough Grammar places for girls** so many went to Secondary Moderns. Girls scores, in the 11+, were also adjusted downwards to allow for boys' 'lower maturity'.

The Comprehensive system introduced in 1960s by the Labour Government, was intended to remove the stigma of failure at 11 and to integrate the social classes, all children in the same neighbourhoods would go to the same school. The fundamental aim of the comprehensive system was **to provide equal opportunities for all pupils, irrespective of class or background – i.e. to be a truly Meritocratic system.**

> **Problems with, and criticisms of, the Comprehensive system**
>
> **Lack of funding**, variety of organisation. The system was introduced 'on the cheap', schools were amalgamated, often on split sites. Planning was poor.
>
> **Some selective schools and all public schools remained** – so it was not really a Comprehensive system.

Schools reflected the localities/neighbourhoods they were built in - some m/c some w/c. So Comprehensive Schools vary greatly in intake and quality of teaching etc, and the hoped for breaking down of social differences (class) has not happened.

Many retained streaming and m/c children were more likely to be put in top streams so in general the inequalities of Tripartite System were reproduced in Comprehensives.

These inequalities led to experiments in **progressive, child-centred education** where children were encouraged to '**discover**' rather than be taught as a class. **Mixed ability** classes was also introduced in some schools, to prevent the inequalities caused by streaming. These developments **were criticised, particularly by the Right, for reducing standards, holding more able children back and producing a lack of discipline in school**

Methods link

Longitudinal Research by the **National Children's Bureau (**of all the children born in a single week in 1958**)** indicates that the brightest 20% did just as well whether they went to Grammar Schools or Comprehensives whilst children of lower ability did somewhat better at Comprehensives than at Secondary Modern Schools.

Longitudinal studies (usually in the form of surveys) are a method that has the ability to **measure changes over time**. We can identify the effects of variables like class, gender and family background on educational performance. For example the NCB survey found that children from single-parent backgrounds tended to achieve lower examination grades, and were more likely to leave school early. **Surveys** such as this have **large samples** and are likely to be **representative**.

However there is a big problem with **sample attrition** – people drop out and, in time this **may make the sample unrepresentative**. Also data collected tends to be quantitative and **does not give us the reasons behind the statistics**. Again if we take the NCB study, though it can tell us that children from single parent families tend to do badly in education, it cannot tell us **why**. Is it because of family structure – lack of a male role model, discipline and support? Or is it because such families often suffer from material deprivation because they are dependent on benefits?

The arguments over Comprehensive Schools continue, but what is clear is that they have not made the differences, in terms of equal opportunities and social integration, that they were intended to. **(See also 'Admissions and Selection' topic).**

Compensatory Education

The Labour government recognised that the home backgrounds of many w/c pupils disadvantaged them in terms of educational success. The research of Functionalist sociologists like **Douglas ('the Home and the School')** had clearly demonstrated the effects of material and cultural deprivation. Compensatory education was aimed at making up for poor home backgrounds. The most famous scheme in the 1960s was in the USA. It was called '**Headstart**' and provided pre-school help for poor children. In Britain **Educational Priority Areas** (in poor neighbourhoods) were established. These got more help/cash and the school day was extended in order to give w/c pupil extra opportunities, facilities and support.

These schemes had only limited success. In Headstart it was found that success was more likely when mothers were involved in schemes but, in general, the schemes got only limited funding and critics argued that '**education cannot compensate for society' (Bernstein**). Limited reforms like this could not make up for the poverty etc that many w/c pupils faced.Compensatory education declined during the Conservative Governments period in office (1979-1997) but was revived by the Labour Government (1997 -2010) **See Labour Reforms (1997-2010) topic, below.**

The New Right - Marketisation and Vocationalism 1979-1997
New Right ideas dominated the educational agenda during this period and, indeed, are still influential today. The **Conservative** government under **Mrs Thatcher** was determined to improve
70

standards through the **marketisation** of education and the **New Vocationalism** that would relate education and training more closely to the needs of the workplace and the economy. The New Right believe in **competition and selection**, though they did not abolish the comprehensive system. The Conservative Government of the 1980s and 90s changed the emphasis in education from inequalities to '**standards**'. The ideology behind this was that schools were failing to provide the training necessary for British workers to be sufficiently skilled to enable Britain to compete with other countries, economically.

The Conservative answer to this was to introduce the **principles of the market place** into education **Competition between schools** was to be encouraged. Parents and pupils were to be '**customers**' or 'clients' and were to be given more '**choice**'.

There were two main themes:

1. The New Vocationalism

There was a new emphasis on skills and business education and new training schemes (work based) for unemployed youngsters e.g. Y.T.S. (now Youth Training) etc. In recent years **GNVQs** (General National Vocational Qualifications / Vocational A-Levels) have being expanded as the vocational equivalent of 4 GCSEs (Intermediate) and 2 A Levels (Advanced). These can be taken in a large number of vocational areas e.g. Business, Social and Healthcare, Information Technology etc. Other aspects of this change to vocational education include the **rapid development of IT and CDT** in schools and schemes like **work experience** etc.

The idea behind these schemes was (and is) to make education and training more related to the world of work and business, to encourage the development of values and skills like **competition and enterprise** and to produce a more highly skilled workforce capable of matching our competitors. It was argued that the failures of education in the 60s and 70s meant that young people often lacked the social as well as technical skills necessary for the world of work.

(See also topic Vocationalism, below)

2.Standards in schools- Marketisation

A number of reforms were introduced, including the merging of CSEs and O-Level GCEs into the current GCSEs (1986). But the most important reforms were initiated by **GERBILL The Great Educational Reform Bill of 1988.**

These reforms included

. **The National Curriculum.**

. **Standard Attainment Tests and Targets** (SATS)

. **Local Financial Management** and opting out of Local Authority control, giving schools more control of their budgets.

. **Open enrolment** – Parental choice of schools – thus 'good' schools can thus take more pupils

. **League Tables** of S.A.T.s, G.C.S.E and "A" Levels.

All these reforms were about "raising standards" through the application of competition to education.

Arguments for the Conservative reforms:

1. **Standardised tests and targets** would help schools, pupils and parents to assess progress and improve standards.

2. **League tables** would allow parents to compare schools which means that they would have the information necessary to choose the best schools for their children

3. **The National Curriculum** would ensure all pupils learn essential knowledge and skills.

4.. **L.F.M. and "Opting Out"** would allow schools to choose how to spend money in the best way for them.

Taken together these measures would mean parents have more information and choice. Good schools can increase intakes and poor schools will have to improve or close.

Arguments against the Conservative reforms

1. The National Curriculum means that the Government has too much control over the Curriculum, "critical" subjects (like Sociology!) were left out.

2. Over emphasis on testing affects what is taught. Pupils now have SATS mocks, and are being taught to pass tests - much time is wasted, especially in Primary Schools.

3. Schools serving poor neighbourhoods would do badly out of 'Open Enrolment' and League Tables do not reflect differences in intake. In fact when these allowances are made many of the top 'selective' schools do badly in comparison with schools in poorer areas.

4. The idea of parents' choice is misleading. It is popular schools who have the choice of pupils. Most parents have little real choice. In fact it is m/c parents who tend to have the choice and influence and what is happening is a return to selection – m/c and w/c schools

See also topic 'Admissions and selection' (below).

1997 - 2010 – The Labour Reforms

Before the 1997 election **Tony Blair** said his priorities were 'education, education, education' and indeed the **Labour government** hugely increased spending on education and brought in a range of reforms. In many ways **Labour continued Conservative, New Right, policies**; though it put more focus on, and increased support for, schools in deprived areas and launched policies to reduce the child poverty that is at the root of much educational failure.

Labour reforms, designed to improve standards included:

1. Emphasis on **SATs, attainment targets**, and regular testing, from the age of 5.

2. **Literacy and Numeracy hours** in Primary Schools to ensure improvements of basic skills (also key skills in Further Education).

3. **Foundation/Specialist schools** which can select some of their pupils according to skills in Arts, Technology, Business etc.

4. **Academies in poor areas** – run by a mixture of business, local groups etc. – these receive extra funding and are allowed to select pupils.

5. **Curriculum 2000** which allowed students to mix academic and vocational A-Levels and were supposed to break down the academic/vocational divide. **In 2008 a new Diploma** started combining Academic and Vocational qualifications, at advanced level.

Other measures have been focussed on improving equality of opportunity/meritocracy and thus improving the performance of the (lower) w/c and 'failing' ethnic minorities.

. **Nursery education for all 3-4 year olds.**

. **Compensatory Education. Education Action Zones** were set up where government and business would fund schools in poor areas – these were not successful (according to inspectors), but have been followed by the introduction of the new '**Academies'**. So far the evidence suggests that these have been somewhat more successful, though critics argue that this is because they have had far more funding than other schools.

. Other ideas like **breakfast and homework clubs, holiday catch-up courses** in the summer holidays for those who are struggling at school, and '**8 to 8' opening in primary schools**.

. The **Surestart** scheme which provides help and support for poor, often single-parent, families as regards education, childcare and work is another major initiative.

. Expansion of Higher Education with a target of 50% to do H.E. courses by 2010

. A big increase in Teaching Assistants to provide help for those with special needs.

2010 Onwards – The Conservative/Liberal coalition reforms

The Coalition government policies can, in may ways, be seen as a continuation of previous policies – especially conservative policies aimed at improving standards and increasing choice and diversity through competition and the application of market principles There is however (at least in theory) a stronger commitment of greater equality of opportunity and improving the educational achievement of the lower social classes. The Coalition government claimed it was committed to reducing inequalities in educational outcomes between rich and poor, particularly through its **pupil premium.** It also believed that educational standards will improve if schools are allowed to be more independent and more diverse in what they offer, hence its **New Academies** and **Free School Policies.**

Let us examine the main Coalition policies:

Government spending on education. The government pledged to maintain school spending, despite the economic recession (an increase of 0.1% above inflation. However, the IFS **(Institute for Fiscal studies),** analysis shows that in **real terms spending per pupil has fallen,** because the 0.1% real terms increase is smaller than the increase in the number of students, and because funding for new academies and Free schools has come out of the same resources.

In addition capital spending (on building etc) has been hugely cut (by 60%) as has non-essential spending. The Institute of Fiscal Studies (IFS) calculates that the spending settlement of 2010 meant that **average spending per pupil fell by by 0.6 per cent a year,** even once the "**pupil premium**" was counted in.

In July 2010 the guillotine fell on the **Building Schools for the Future** programme and by December the £3,290 maximum charge on university fees had been raised to £9,000. **The Pupil Premium** gave poorer children e.g. those on free school meals an extra £488 per head in 2011, rising to £623 in 2012 and £900 in 2013, but the Coalition abolished the Education Maintenance Allowance (EMA), which had given sixth formers from poor families some £30 a week to help them continue studying, replacing it with a much more limited bursary scheme.

Academies and Free schools – Increasing choice and diversity 'Better schools for all' The Coalition encouraged **all schools to apply for academy status,** starting with 'outstanding schools'. These new Academies have included many selective/grammar schools and are free of local government control (and receive extra resources). **Critics** argue that granting Academy status to outstanding schools misses the point in terms of addressing educational inequality. The majority of the new wave of academies introduced by Michael Gove have good or outstanding Ofsteds and are often located in middle class areas. There are now over 3000 academies, accounting for over half of all secondary schools and six per cent of primaries. Academies began under Labour as a way to replace failing comprehensives in deprived areas, with schools benefiting from extra funding, often with support from businesses and other sponsors and extra funding, often with extensive new buildings, new heads, uniforms and strict discipline policies, plus plenty of support and monitoring. The Coalition has greatly expanded this programme arguing that giving such schools greater freedom and independence will encourage diversity and choice and drive up standards,

Such schools have more control over spending and don't have to buy services from the local authorities. Academies also have the freedom to control the length of terms and days, plus teachers' pay and conditions, and to opt out of the national curriculum — though only within limits, as they are still subject to Ofsted inspections and national targets. They are even allowed to employ unqualified teachers. All new maintained schools have to be academies or free schools.

There have been many criticisms of the 'New Academies'. Some belong to chains, e.g. Harris, Ark etc which may be large — the largest, the Academies Enterprise Trust, runs over 70. In March the DFE announced that it was barring AET from taking over more schools because of concerns that its rapid expansion was hitting standards. The chain has also been criticised for paying nearly £500,000 into the private business interests of its trustees and executives. There have been accusations of fraud and instances of financial mismanagement and extravagance because of a lack of monitoring.

Critics also argue that there is evidence that some academies have manipulated the admissions process to raise their results, e.g. by limiting the number of children with special needs and those on free school meals.

The coalition also encouraged the setting up of **'Free Schools',** again outside local authority control and run by parents, businesses, charities, businesses, universities, existing schools, community, educational and faith groups (the last can select up to 50 per cent of pupils on the basis of religion) etc. the government claims that this will help raise standards. However the evidence from Sweden, where such schools have operated for over a decade, suggests free schools failed to improve standards, and that the policy there increased social segregation (class divisions). Again it is only better off (m/c and u/c) parents who have the cultural and material capital to be able to set up such schools. The free schools programme has also been criticised for a lack of transparency about costs, there has been a large-scale waste of money particularly when planned schools have failed to open. Some have opened in areas with a surplus of places in existing schools, at a time when there is a growing shortage of primary school places nationally; others have opened despite being under-subscribed by up to 50 per cent. They have also to take their fair share of the poorest children. There are also concerns that some schools (Religious Schools) may encourage extremist views, because of the lack of effective monitoring of Free Schools.

The evidence regarding the success of the Academies and Free School programme is inconclusive. However a Parliamentary report to the Government in 2015 concluded that there was 'no evidence that Academies and Free Schools had improved educational standards'.

Critics argue that, in general, greater diversity and choice tends to advantage those (m/c) families who have the cultural capital to make choices, and the material capital to move near the best schools. What we will be left with is a two tier system – the academies and free schools with higher status and attracting m/c pupils and the local authority schools with far less status and largely w/c intakes.

The Pupil Premium One of the main policies of the Liberals before the 2010 General Election was the 'pupil premium'. The idea was to encourage 'good schools' to take in pupils from poor backgrounds by giving them extra money for such pupils. As part of a £7bn package schools were to receive additional funds to offer targeted help to every pupil eligible for Free School Meals. The idea being to provide help to the poorest pupils. However the IFS argues that this will not be the case because this money will come from cuts elsewhere, and that anyway 'good schools' will only select the most able pupils from poor backgrounds so as not to affect their league table positions.

The curriculum and the 'English Baccalaureate' The Coalition government has said that it wishes to free schools from government control of the curriculum. At the same time however it is encouraging the adoption of the **'English Baccalaureate'.** In the league tables this means that school success at GCSE will be measured by the number of pupils who gain C or above grades in English, Maths, Sciences, a Foreign Language and Humanities (but only Geography and History) this will, in effect , force most schools to make all students take a foreign language and either history or geography so as to maintain their positions in the League tables.

Critics argue this is government control by 'the back door' and that other subjects – Arts, Music, and of course Sociology, will be devalued and indeed dropped by many schools.

GCSEs and A-Levels have been reformed. From 2015 onwards students will take two year A-Level Courses with exams at the end of the second year (instead of the previous modular system). They can also take AS-level courses, worth half an A-Level, but of the same standard. GCSE coursework will be severely restricted. The argument behind these changes is that A-Level and GCSE exams have become easier, grades have been inflated and standards have suffered.

Post 16 education

The coalition abolished Educational Maintenance Grants. EMAs were introduced by the Labour Govt to provide support for post compulsory education age students from poorer families to continue their studies. A weekly allowance of between £30 and £10 was payable to 16-18 year old students on full time courses EMAs are now to be phased out, though (see above) money has been found for students with the most desperate need. The impact of this change is still unclear, but it may well have dissuaded many poor young people from continuing in full time post 16 education.

Higher education

The government has pushed through plans to allow universities to charge up to £9,000 per year, raising the cap from its previous level of £3,290. Universities wanting to charge more than £6,000 would have to undertake measures, such as offering bursaries, summer schools and outreach programmes, to encourage students from poorer backgrounds to apply. The government will continue to loan students the money for fees. The threshold at which graduates have to start paying their loans back would be raised from £15,000 to £21,000. In reality almost all Universities are charging £9,000 and debts upon leaving are likely to be £40,000 plus..

Critics argue that it is likely that many poorer students and even those from the 'squeezed middle' (m/c and w/c families who whilst not poor are also not rich!) will be put off by such high rates of debt. The policy has caused mass student protests.

Changes and reforms - Evaluation

If we look at the main thrust of educational changes since 1944 we can see that the aims have been:-
1. **To improve standards and skills** - to produce a more skilled and productive workforce.
2. **To increase meritocracy** – produce an education system that gives equal opportunities to all irrespective of class, ethnicity or gender.
So how successful have reforms been?

Standards

1. There is plenty of evidence to show that achievement has improved. The numbers of students taking, and passing GCSEs, A-Levels and degrees has more than doubled in the past 20 years.
2. SATS results show improvements in both numeracy and literacy – especially in Primary Schools.

However:-

1. Critics argue that GCSEs, A-Levels and Degrees have been made easier – **grade inflation**, and that vocational qualifications are of a low standard. For example many 'low achieving' schools have adopted GCSE level GNVQ courses in Business, IT etc which, if passed, give students the equivalent of 4 GCSEs at grade C or above. Critics argue that these courses are of a lower standard than GCSE and make GCSE results look better. The Coalition reforms of exams (see above) are a reaction to such criticisms).
2. Employers (and universities) have complained about low standards of literacy, numeracy etc. amongst undergraduate students. Some Universities now have their own entrance tests because they say A-Level results have been inflated, and do not provide a good guide as to who are the most able students.
3. Critics also argue that SATs results have improved not because pupils have become more skilled in Maths, Science and English, but because they are being taught to pass the tests!

Meritocracy?

1. There is no doubt that **girls** have made enormous strides – overtaking boys in achievement **BUT** they are still far less likely to do sciences, maths and other high status/high paid subjects (and jobs afterwards).
2. Though many **Asians have improved performance** and do as well or better than whites some **groups are still left behind – especially male West Indians.** Class remains a big issue in both gender and ethnic inequalities - lower w/c girls still achieve poor results and many Ethnic Minorities come from poor w/c families with high levels of unemployment.
3. **Class differences remain.** Although overall achievement has risen significantly the **success gap** between w/c and m/c has not decreased e.g. although more lower w/c pupils are going to University (in 2000 13%) the increase in pupils with professional backgrounds at university is even greater (in 2000 72%). In fact **upward social mobility** (moving from w/c to m/c) has decreased over the past 20 years.

How do we explain this? As **Bernstein** said "Education cannot compensate for society". There is still patriarchy in society and many w/c and ethnic minorities suffer from material and cultural disadvantages which stem from poverty – changes in education alone cannot fix this.

Note: When answering questions on educational reforms be very careful about the time period specified. If you are asked about educational reforms over the past 25 years it is no good rambling on about comprehensives!

Key issues in education today
Selection and admissions

There has always been great debate about the means by which pupils are assigned to schools. Should students be selected, on the basis of ability? Or should pupils go to their neighbourhood schools – as was the comprehensive ideal? Even when comprehensive schools were introduced selection, on various grounds, remained.

Religion

There have always been Religious Schools in Britain. Before 1870 charity and church schools were the only schools available to poor children. When 'Faith schools' were incorporated into the State system they were allowed to continue to select pupils on a faith basis. In recent years Governments have restated their belief in faith schools, and indeed have encouraged the formation of new religious schools, arguing that they generally achieve high standards and allow parents choice. Also faith schools are seen to be linked to local communities and to encourage the development of strong, positive, values. At present Moslem schools are increasing, the first Hindu state school opened in 2008.

Critics argue that communities should not be divided on religious grounds. Such segregation is likely to produce greater ethnic divisions. Moreover they provide another means for m/c parents to use their **cultural (and material capital)** to get their children into 'better performing schools'. This is supported by a **Government financed study of 96 schools released by then Education Minister Ed Balls (2008)** which found that one in six state funded schools broke admissions guidelines, by asking for financial contributions (up to £895 per term) from parents, as well as bank and other financial details. **The worst culprits were faith schools.**

The introduction of **Free Schools** has boosted the number of religious schools. About ¼ of Free schools are religious. Most are Christian but a number of Moslem and Sikh schools have also been opened. There have been concerns over such schools teaching things like creationism and also encouraging religious intolerance. At the Al Madinah Moslem School in Derby all females were

76

forced to wear head scarves and the sexes were segregated. An Ofsted inspection found the school to be 'dysfunctional'. Eventually the school was closed down. Similarly the Christian Durham Free School was closed down after an Ofsted inspection found it to be inadequate in all areas. In such schools it is argued religion is considered more important than education.

Ability

The Tripartite system was, of course based on selection by ability but, as we have seen, the selection process was flawed and unfair on w/c students and girls. The 11+ test was culturally biased favouring m/c children and girls had to achieve higher scores to gain Grammar School places (there were also less selective places for girls). Despite comprehensivisation some LEAs, like Kent, maintain Grammar Schools and Public Schools, which select pupils on the basis of ability to pay, remain. Selection has indeed made a comeback. Specialist Schools (i.e. those who specialise in Languages, Science, IT etc.) are allowed to select up to 10% of their intake.

The arguments in favour of selection by ability also apply to streaming and setting in schools:

1. It means pupils are able to work at their own pace. The more able are not held back by the less able and low ability children are not made to feel inferior by the more able.

2. It is also easier and more efficient to teach pupils of similar ability.

3. Specialist schools give talented students the facilities and opportunities to excel in their chosen fields.

There are however strong arguments against admission by selection:

1. Selection tests and procedures are flawed and biased. (see above)

2. Pupils who fail selection tests are effectively labelled as failures and often give up. (SFP)

3. Specialist schools have better funding and facilities than non-selective schools.

Neighbourhood Schools and Catchment areas

One of the original aims of comprehensivisation was to move away from admission by ability and mix children of different backgrounds and abilities. They were to be neighbourhood schools where pupils from a particular (catchment area) all attended the same school.

The advantages of such an approach include:

1. The school is linked to the community and encourages social integration of pupils of similar backgrounds.

2. Equal opportunities irrespective of ability and background.

3. An end to the negative effects of selection – labelling, SFP etc

There were however problems with the practical implementation of these ideals from the very start:

1. Selection remained in many areas.

2. Schools were of very different qualities from the start. They tended to reflect the neighbourhoods in which they were situated. In crude terms poor w/c estates tended to have poorer quality schools.

3. Over the years this problem has worsened as m/c parents have used their cultural capital to get their children places in the 'best' comprehensive schools. So the 'good comprehensives' have become better (and more m/c) whilst those of lower quality have deteriorated as the 'able m/c' pupils have 'moved out'.

Parental Choice

From the 1980s onwards 'parental choice' became the basis of admission procedures – though this was more in theory than in fact. The 'New Right' argued that standards could only be improved by the marketisation of education. Parents (and their children) would be 'consumers' and the laws of supply and demand would be applied to schools. The Conservative government argued that this would mean that 'good schools could increase their numbers, through '**open enrolment**' whilst

77

'bad schools would have to improve or close' (because most parents would not send their children to such schools). The Free Schools and Academies programme has increased the focus on parental choice.Parents would make **informed decisions based on league tables and OFSTED (inspection) reports**. The Labour government maintained this policy and, through the expansion of specialist schools and provision of Academies, has actually increased choice.

Critics, however argue that the issue of choice is irrelevant to most parents and misleading. M/c parents are far more likely to be able to manipulate the situation (see studies below) and achieve their choices. Nor do League tables truly reflect school achievements. Schools in poorer catchment areas with a high proportion of poor w/c and ethnic minority students are bound to be less successful in terms of exam results because of their intake. In effect it is popular successful schools that have the choice of pupils (not the parents) because they are over-subscribed.

These developments are clearly illustrated by two studies:

Gerwitz, Ball and Bowe 1995, interviewed parents about the way they made decisions over which schools to send their children to. They found that m/c parents were far more skilled in using the system for their children's benefit. They were more likely to use the appeals system, arrange interviews with heads and use contacts (Governors, teachers etc.) to ensure they got their first choice school. W/c parents tended to be 'disconnected choosers' they did not have the skills or knowledge to make informed choices or to use the system to their children's benefit.

It is not however merely a case of cultural capital. The greater wealth of m/c parents is also important. **Gibbons and Machin (2006)** studied house prices in the South East. They found that houses in 'good catchment areas' sold for up to £61,000 more than the same houses in areas with less successful schools. This development has been described as a kind of 'selection by mortgage'. Note also that m/c parents are more likely to make financial contributions to 'buy' their way into 'good schools' (see faith schools, above).

Balancing Intakes – Banding

One solution to the complex question of admissions has been **banding.** The idea is that children are given aptitude tests before they enter school. On the basis of their results they are assigned to three bands (higher, middle and lower). Each school in the area is then given a balanced intake/mixture of abilities from each three bands.

This is obviously a fairer system in that it gives all children, irrespective of ability and background, the chance to enjoy a similar quality of education. Although it can be argued that such tests still result in labelling, this does not result in children being assigned to different schools, based on their ability. It should also, in theory, prevent m/c parents from using the system in their favour. In this however lies one of the biggest problems. It works against the interests of parents (especially m/c parents) who want to ensure that their children get the best possible school. It restricts their choice. Some m/c parents have even taken their children out of the state system in response to this policy.

Admissions policy – a lottery?

Brighton Council has come up with an innovative idea to tackle these problems.- the idea of a lottery. Brighton is divided into six catchment areas and pupils will go to a school within their local area. However when a school is over-subscribed who gets the places will be decided by a lottery. Thus all pupils, irrespective of ability and background, will have the same chance of getting into the school of their choice. Many residents have welcomed this change but others have strongly opposed it, as being against the principle of choice – much of the opposition has come from m/c parents.

Test your knowledge and understanding

1. What criticisms have been made of the admissions procedures of 'religious schools'?

2. Give two arguments for and two against neighbourhood schools.

3. Give two problems associated with 'parental choice'. In what ways can 'banding' be seen as a fairer method of admissions/selection?

Non-Governmental influence and involvement in education

> **Learning objectives**
>
> 1.Knowledge and understanding of the role of non-government organisations in education – Religious groups, Public Schools and Business-financed schools.
>
> 2. Analysis and evaluation of the role of non-government organisations.

Faith Schools

As we have already noted Faith schools have been an important element in State Education since its inception. Traditionally most of these schools have been Christian although there have always been a small number of Jewish schools and now Moslem Schools and to a lesser extent Hindu, Sikh and Buddhist schools are being introduced and planned.

Supporters of Faith Schools argue that:

. People should have the **freedom to choose** an education that is in tune with their religious beliefs and values.

. Faith Schools tend to achieve **higher standards**, in terms of exam results etc. than other state schools.

.**Standards of behaviour are higher** because of the religious beliefs and values that they are based on.

. Faith schools help to **preserve the cultures of minority groups** and provide a haven from the discrimination and racism they might otherwise face.

Critics argue that:

. **Faith Schools are divisive and prevent integration**. Children should not be segregated on the basis of faith in a multicultural society – such a policy is likely to produce tension and conflict.

. The 'higher standards' of faith schools reflect the fact that many m/c parents try to ensure that their children go to such school (by attending church etc.) .As we have already seen many **faith schools are guilty of flouting admissions policies** and 'requesting' money from parents in order for their children to attend.

. **In other countries, for example France, religion is 'kept out of the classroom'**. Indeed France even banned the wearing of headscarves and other religious symbols. The argument is that children should be exposed to a variety of belief systems and allowed to make up their own minds.

. Some faith groups have also become involved in the Government 'City Academies' scheme and concerns have been expressed at such groups being able to **push through their 'religious agendas in these 'flagship' state schools**. The businessman Reg Vardy, for example ,has been involved in setting up two such schools and is planning others. He is a fundamentalist Christian and his schools have been accused of teaching 'Creationism' and 'Intelligent Design' in Science rather than RE lessons where, critics argue, they belong.

The Coalition Governments policy of encouraging **'Free Schools'** is likely to encourage more Religious Schools, many of the first Free Schools opened since 2011 are indeed 'religious schools'.

The Independent/'Public' schools.

Throughout the post-war period Independent Schools have remained immune from most Government reforms. This is because they are not State Schools and so are not financed by taxes. Independent Schools charge fees to some or all pupils. Most famous are so-called Public Schools eg Harrow, Eton and Westminster who traditionally prepared pupils for Public Office (there are about 200 of these). 7% of all pupils go to Independent Schools, though 18% of boys and 15% of girls 16 and over attend these institutions.

> **The advantages of Independent Schools, for those who attend them, are:**
>
> **Smaller class sizes.**
>
> **Better facilities**- libraries, IT, Games Fields etc.

> **Highly qualified teachers** (usually from higher class backgrounds, and often better paid than those in the state sector).
>
> **"The Old School tie"** system of informal contacts gives huge advantages in application for top jobs and Universities.
>
> **The Academic ethos** and **hidden curriculum** that encourages high achievement and leadership qualities. Many pupils who attend are boarders and receive intensive education, including evening 'prep'.

Supporters of public schools argue that people should have the right to pay for their children's education if they so wish and that public schools set an example of high standards. Indeed the Labour Government and its Coalition successor have tried to form 'partnerships' between state and public schools to use public school expertise.

Critics argue these schools are elitist and socially divisive. The vast majority of those who attend are from Upper Class and "top" professional backgrounds. They perpetuate privilege and snobbery.

Marxists would argue that this is a classic example of Cultural Reproduction and indeed of how education reproduces the class system.

Public Domain Image Public Schools have long been a contentious issue in Britain. Public school pupils are still five times as likely to get to University as those from State Schools

Business

Right from the beginnings of compulsory state education there has been a focus on the need to produce workers with the necessary skills to maintain a competitive economy. The increasing pace of economic globalisation and free trade has added to this concern. The 1988 Educational reform Act as well as putting a new emphasis on the 'New Vocationalism' established **City Technology Colleges**. The Labour government was, if anything, been even more keen to get business involved in schools. **Trust Schools** and the new '**Academies**' were both supposed to be part-financed by private business (at a level of 10%), as well as getting involved in the running and ethos of these schools – bringing in values of enterprise and business. Under the Coalition and Conservative governments businesses were encouraged to be far more involved in supporting both the 'New Academies' and Free Schools.

The **evidence** in terms of the benefits of these innovations is, at present, contradictory and limited (Academies are a new innovation). Inspectors reports and exam results, however, do point to some improvements, in academies at least.

These developments are criticised on two levels. Firstly many critics are uneasy at the growing business interests in schools arguing that the focus on 'work skills' will result in a narrowing of the curriculum and a failure to cover other aspects of education – culture, the arts etc. Secondly the 'improvements' are disputed. These schools have received higher funding, and are able to be more selective. It is also likely that m/c parents have switched their children to these schools because of the better facilities that they offer.

Test your understanding

1. Outline the reasons why many parents wish to send their children to faith schools.

2. What criticisms can be made of faith schools?

3. Why are some parents willing to pay to send their children to public schools?

4. Why are some sociologists critical of public schools?

5. Why have governments, in recent years, encouraged business involvement in state schools?

6. What criticisms can be made of business involvement in state schools.

Vocational Education

Learning objectives

1. Knowledge and understanding of the nature and development of vocational education in Britain.

.2. Analysis and evaluation of changes in vocational education in Britain.

Vocational education in Britain has never had the status that it has in countries like Germany, where vocational schools and degree courses are well established and are considered as important as academic courses. As we have seen compulsory education was first introduced in order to produce a skilled, literate and numerous workforce. Under the tripartite system Technical Schools were set up, but never in sufficient quantities, when compared with grammar and secondary modern schools. The New Vocationalism of the 1980s and 90s brought in a new range of courses which replaced the old apprenticeship, 'training on the job', system. These included **Youth Training, GNVQs and NVQs and Key Skills, amongst other developments**. The Labour party, when it came to power re-branded GNVQs as 'Applied A-levels' and introduced '**Curriculum 2000**' which encouraged 16 year old students to 'pick and mix' academic and vocational A-Levels. New diplomas have also been introduced which also allow students to 'mix' qualifications at the post-16 level.

All of these changes have been designed to relate education and training more closely to the world of work and the needs of employers. But there have always been problems of '**parity of esteem'.** Academic qualifications have always been more highly regarded by students, parents and employers.

The arguments in favour of vocational education, in a technological age, are clear. To be successful economies need to have technically qualified workers and education needs to serve the needs of the economy, especially as low skilled jobs are being moved to cheap labour economies as globalisation proceeds at a dramatic rate. However the vocational reforms introduced by successive governments have come under strong criticism, mostly from Marxists and other radical critics.

Criticisms of Vocational Education

The system is **divisive** - education for the elite, training for the rest.

Extending vocational education and training has been **more about keeping down the unemployment figures than improving skills**. Anyway the assumption that young people are unemployed through lack of skills is demonstrably wrong, they are unemployed because of lack of jobs!

Schemes like Y.T. are more about **social control and producing a conformist, obedient. workforce** than about real training, "keeping bums on seats and off the streets". **Willis (1984)** found a big emphasis on 'Social Education' - punctuality, dress, obedience etc. **Cohen** argued that such schemes were skill destroying not creating - apprenticeships were destroyed by YT.

Many training schemes and G.N.V.Q.s are criticised for being of a **very low standard.**

Y.T. etc has **driven down wage levels and produced cheap labour** for Capitalism.

Test your knowledge and understanding

Produce a brain map of the arguments for and against government policies on vocational education in Britain.

Post-compulsory education

Learning objectives

1. Knowledge and understanding of changes and reforms to post compulsory education over the past twenty years

2. Evaluation of government policies relating to post-compulsory education

Post-compulsory education consists of all education that students receive after the age of 16, though in practice the vast majority of young people continue education or training after this age.

Schools, Tertiary Colleges and Further Education.

Most students continue their post-16 education in Schools or in Colleges of Further Education. In some areas however there are only Tertiary Colleges, which all post-16 students attend. All these institutions offer a range of courses. In schools A-Levels predominate, and choices, especially in smaller schools, tend to be limited. Further and Tertiary Education Colleges tend to offer a broader range of courses, including vocational courses.

Successive Governments have attempted to encourage the development of vocational courses to encourage 'less academic pupils to go on to further education (see above), but thus far with limited success, though the introduction of the new **Post-16 Diplomas** may change this. The Labour Government also tried to encourage, particularly w/c students, to stay on in education after the age of 16 by providing Educational Maintenance Allowances (**EMAs),** of up to £30 per week for the less well off students. The number of students staying on in Post-16 education has dramatically increased over the last 20 years and now the government has introduced compulsory education or training until the age of eighteen.

Higher Education

There has also been a dramatic increase in the number of students attended Universities and other forms of Higher Education. The Labour Government set a target of 50% of young people (under the age of thirty) in Higher Education by 2010. When one considers that in the 1960s only 6.5% of children went to university this is indeed a dramatic rise.

Of course the cost of this **widening participation** has been high and the Government in England has introduced Tuition Fees, on the grounds that those who benefit from Higher Education should contribute towards its cost. Although some, poor, students can attain Grants, most Students now have to take out loans and critics have argued that many bright w/c students have been 'put off' going to University by the prospect of the huge debts they will face at the end of their course. **Callender and Jackson (2005)** tested this proposition by giving **questionnaires** to a **stratified sample** of prospective University students. They found that those poorer students were more worried about debts. In further research they also found that poorer students left University with, on average, significantly bigger debts than those from more affluent backgrounds (who tend to receive greater financial support from parents).

The Labour Government was very conscious of these criticisms and attempted to encourage more

82

poor, w/c, students to attend Universities by encouraging Universities to take more students from such backgrounds, and through the **Aim Higher Scheme** which provides resources for schools to use to encourage pupils to go to University.

There are other criticisms of Labours policies, however. **The 'New Right'** tend to argue that widening participation has cause a **lowering of standards**. It is far easier to get to University now and far easier to get a good degree.

The Coalition's increase in University tuition fees (up to £9,000) increased financial pressures on students and may lead to those with lower/middle incomes being more reluctant to go to University, though the Coalition argue that the future rewards for those who take degrees more than compensates for short-term debt. In addition students do not have to start repaying the debt until their income surpasses the average wage. This leads to another problem: it is estimated that over 40% of students will never repay their debt.

Official Statistics show that the proportion of pupils who go to University from the higher social classes (non-manual) is much higher than those from lower social classes (manual) – almost 50% compared to less than 20%. The gap between the Professional classes and Unskilled manual workers is even greater. The child of a professional couple is five times more likely to go to University than the child of an unskilled manual worker.

Test your knowledge and understanding

1. In what ways have governments encouraged wider participation in post-compulsory education? Why have they done this?

2. Why did the Labour Government introduce 'Tuition Fees'?

3. What criticisms have been made of Labour policies relating to Higher Education?

4. Outline the arguments for and against the Coalitions decision to increase tuition fees.

AS and A-Level exam type questions and tips

Both AS and A-Level exams require students to answer short questions. These do not necessarily have to be answered in full sentences.

Examples of AS short questions:

The first question requires a short definition/explanation:
1. Define the term 'material deprivation'. (2 marks)
2. Define the term 'labelling' (2 marks)
So for Q1 you might write something like '**Lacking the physical resources – e.g. Poor housing, poor diet, lack of books etc. needed to succeed in education**' Be careful not to repeat the word used in the question – **i.e.** Lacking the **material** resources!

The second question requires a brief explanation:
1. Using one example, briefly explain how material deprivation may effect educational achievement. (2 marks)
2, Using one example, briefly explain how the 'negative labelling' may affect educational achievement. (2 marks)
So for Q2 you might write something like '**If a child is labelled as unintelligent they may accept that label and so give up and fail'. For Q1 'If a family can't afford the books and equipment needed to support their child the child may fail/fall behind in school.**

Examples of A-Level Short questions:

The first question on the A-Level paper requires you to make two brief points/explanations:
1. Outline two material factors that may affect social class differences differences in social class achievement. (4 marks)
2. Outline two school factors that may negatively affect the educational achievement of boys. (4 marks)
For this type of questions brief answers are required e.g. For Q1 you might write:
'If a family can't afford decent housing and the house is damp children may suffer more ill health and so have more time off school and fall behind'
"If a family can't afford books, computers etc their children may find it difficult to do homework etc and so fall behind better off children'
Note that you do not need to go into any depth – a brief answer is all that is required.

Q3 on the AS paper and Q2 on the A-Level paper are the same in terms of wording and what is required to produce a good answer. Examples:
1. Outline three reasons why government education policies aimed at raising educational achievement amongst disadvantaged groups may not always succeed. (6 marks)
2. Outline three ways in which home factors may negatively affect the achievement of some ethnic minorities. (6 marks)
Again such questions only require a brief answer. So for Q2 you might write:
'Some ethnic groups, such as Pakistanis may have English as a second language and so not speak English at home, this can disadvantage the children in school because their English skills may be limited'
'New Right sociologists argue that, because many Afro-Caribbean families are female-headed, single parent, families boys lack a fathers discipline at home and so behave badly at school and suffer more from negative labelling, suspensions and expulsions which limits their attendance and achievement'

84

'Some ethnic minorities e.g Pakistanis and Bengalese may send their children back to their country of origin to maintain links to their wider family and culture. This means they miss school at crucial times, sometimes for long periods, thus disrupting their schooling'

You would probably get two marks for writing less than this but try to make sure you get the full marks by giving a brief explanation.

Q4 on the AS paper is a ten mark question. You are required to outline and explain two points/reasons etc. Obviously this requires a greater depth of explanation that previous questions.

Examples of AS Q4:

1. Outline and explain two reasons for gender differences in subject choice. (10 marks)
2. Outline and explain two reasons why working class pupils are more likely to join anti-school subcultures, (10 marks)

To gain full marks you need to identify a reason and then explain/analyse it in some detail. You could also add a little evaluation. For Q1, for example, your answer might be:

'One reason for differences in subject choice may be primary socialisation (this identifies a reason, now you have to explain it) Boys are socialised by parents into being more active and physical whereas girls are expected to be more passive and less adventurous. This leads to girls developing a 'bedroom culture' and thus they spend more time reading and talking with friends, thus developing their language skills, Girls are thus attracted to subjects that enable them to use these skills – English Language and Literature and foreign languages for example, whereas boys tend to choose more 'hands on' subjects like physics and IT. This however may be changing. There have been numerous changes in the curriculum – e.g. All children now have to take sciences at GCSE so girls are no longer able to opt out of such subjects'

Note that this answer fully explains why subject choice are different. It analyses the reason. It does not simply describe it. Note also the final sentence which includes some evaluation – outlining an argument that differences in subject choice may be changing.

Q4 (A-Level), Q5 (AS) is an **Evaluation/Assessment essay** – analysing the strengths and weaknesses, pros and cons, advantages and disadvantages of a particular theory/issue etc. On the AS paper this essay is worth 20 marks on the A-Level paper 30 marks, though the structure and demands of the questions are the same. You will be given a short item to apply to your answer but will mostly have to use your own knowledge. Look at the following examples:

1. Applying material from Item A and your knowledge, evaluate the view that education is functional for the individual and society.

2. Applying material from Item A and your knowledge, evaluate the view that educational underachievement by many w/c pupils is the result of home and family background influences.

You must use the item in this question – and develop points from it – don't just copy chunks out. Also don't forget theory and concepts!

Let us look at how you would go about answering the first question (above). Obviously this is a Functionalist viewpoint so you need to state this in your first paragraph. You then need to explain the Functionalist perspective – Durkheim Parsons, Davis and Moore etc. and clearly explain what they see as the functions of education for society **and the individual.** To get top marks you need to focus on the individual as well as society as a whole. Let's look at an example.

'Functionalists argue that the education system is responsible for secondary socialisation - teaching pupils the norms and values of wider society, so that we all share the same values (value

consensus). Durkheim argues that this produces social solidarity and helps to maintain social order in society. This also benefits the individual, people need order and stability in their lives and to feel a sense of belonging.'

Of course this is an evaluation/assessment question. To get high marks **you need to evaluate on a point by point basis – not just explain functionalist theory and then simply state what other theories have to say.**

Let us look at how we might assess the point above:

Marxists, however, argue that the educational system is not functional for society and the individual but for capitalism and the ruling class. Althusser argues that education is part of the Ideological State Apparatus and far from teaching common values, teaches ideology – the values and beliefs of the ruling class...

To get high marks on this question it is a very good idea to practise this point by point evaluation technique. You will not be required to evaluate every point you make but three or four developed evaluations of arguments/evidence/theory will enable you to get high marks.

Q5 on the A-Level paper is a methods in context question. We will look at this, and the equivalent AS question, at the end of the Methods section.

TOPIC 3 - SOCIOLOGY METHODS FINDING OUT ABOUT SOCIETY

Sociological research – finding out about society.
Methodology

> **Learning objectives**
>
> 1. Knowledge and understanding of the general nature of and issues regarding methodology.
>
> 2. Knowledge and understanding of the differences between primary and secondary and quantitive and qualitative methods/data.
>
> 3. Knowledge and understanding of the relationships between theory and methodology.

Methodology is the study of methods. At its simplest it is the study of the methods used to collect data – e.g. questionnaires and interviews, the strengths and weaknesses of different methods and the accuracy of the data they produce.
There are other questions though – over ethics, and why certain methods may be chosen. Theory and practical issues are also important.

Important, basic, stuff:

> **We can divide methods into:**
>
> **Primary sources/methods** which relate to data that was not present when the researcher stated his/her research i.e. it is data that the researcher produces herself through questionnaires etc.
>
> **Secondary sources**/methods on the other hand refer to data that already exists – produced by other sociologists or government reports, personal documents, mass media texts etc.
>
> **We can also divide methods into:-**
>
> **Quantitative methods/data which** is simply data that can be put into numbers. It can be measured – questionnaires and structured interviews often produce this kind of measurable data.
>
> **Qualitative methods/data** focuses more on meanings and feelings which cannot be expressed in numbers – methods like participant observation and unstructured interviews produce this kind of data.

Theory and methods

Positivist/structuralist sociologists prefer to use quantitative methods. This is because they believe human behaviour is the product of the structures of society "society makes wo/man". There are "laws of social behaviour", just as there are natural laws. Because we are made to behave in certain ways behaviour is predictable and can be measured. Thus quantitative methods are used to establish the facts, test hypotheses and produce theories.
Interpretive/interactionist sociologists, however, take an "anti-positivist approach". There are no laws of social behaviour. It is people who create society and it's structures through everyday interaction with others. "wo/man makes society" and has choices in how they behave. Thus qualitative methods must be used because to understand peoples behaviour we have to be able to "get inside their heads" and see the world as they see it. Feminists also tend to prefer qualitative methods. They see the positivist approach as being male biased – "patriarchal". And want to use methods which allow women "to tell their own stories".
Of course in practice sociologists often choose a variety of methods to get the "numbers" and "meanings". This is called methodological pluralism.

Sociology and Science

Sociology is a "Social Science" along with Psychology, Economics and Law (etc.) It attempts to study and explain peoples' behaviour in a logical and systematic way. But is it "scientific"? The short answer to this is, that it depends what you mean by Science!

A simple definition of Science is that it is knowledge that can be proved – **verifiable knowledge**, and as Sociology produces theories, does research and uses evidence to test theories, in this sense it can be called a Science. It is, however, a bit more complicated than this:

The Positivist/Structuralist Approach

The Founding Fathers of Sociology – Marx, Durkheim, and to a lesser extent Weber took it for granted that Sociology was a science. **Marx and Durkheim** based their study of society on the Natural Sciences and believed there were **Social Laws and Facts** which are external to human beings "Laws of human behaviour which people have to follow" just like the Law of Gravity or Natural Selection. We call this a **Positivist** approach.

We should be seeking to discover these **laws** and **facts**, in an **objective** and **value free** way – research should not be influenced by the researcher's opinions or values and the researcher must be **detached** (removed/apart) from the subjects of his/her research.

Experiments/research should be **reliable** i.e. if the research is repeated in the same way **(replicated)** the same results should be obtained. The results should be **quantitative** i.e. easily made into figures so that **hypotheses** and **theories** can be tested and **correlations** and **causes/causality** established. Results should be **representative** of the group studied i.e. they should reflect the social make-up of the group in terms of class, age, gender etc. Positivist sociologists often use very large samples, thousands of people can be studied through questionnaires etc. Research should be **systematic** – follow set procedures - so that the researcher doesn't influence the results. For all these reasons quantitative methods/sources are preferred.

A very important part of ensuring objectivity is the **publication** of results. This enables other sociologists to check both the method and the results for mistakes or bias.

The Interpretive/Interactionist Approach

Interpretive sociologists argue that sociology cannot be scientific in the same way as natural science because we are dealing with people. This is, in one way, an advantage as they can answer our questions and tell us things – unlike animals, plants and inanimate objects. On the other hand people are conscious beings who have **choices** about how they behave and react. Interpretive Sociologists argue that to really understand why people behave as they do we need to "get inside their heads" and understand how they see their behaviour – what **meanings** they attach to it - e.g. A person steps in front of a bus. We cannot know **why** he did it without knowing what he was thinking at the time.

This leads us to the key Interpretive criticism of Positivist/Scientific approaches. The sort of methods used by such Sociologists lack **validity** they do not produce true to life results – in experiments people may not behave naturally, because its an artificial situation and they know it – they are conscious beings. Similarly they may not give accurate, honest answers to Questionnaires. Often people will give the answers or behave in the way they think the experimenter wants them to (**demand characteristics**).

Interpretive Sociologists therefore argue that you must use methods which "get inside peoples heads" and help you to **empathise** (see the world from their point of view) a process Weber called **verstehen;** methods such as Participant Observation and unstructured interviews which allow people to give their "**meanings and feelings**". This allows you to get much more **depth and detail** than using questionnaires etc (though it means that samples may be small and **unrepresentative**). You cannot be detached, indeed, you must be **involved** in order to really understand your subjects. Similarly you cannot really be objective for the same reason

In more recent years a **Realist** approach has been developed. This accepts that to explain human behaviour you need to understand their consciousness but it also argues that there are structures and mechanisms in society that constrain human behaviour. So you have to examine both. Sociology

88

cannot be scientific in the way that Physics is, but it can produce models and theories to explain how the social world works, and test and amend these in the light of evidence.

Test your understanding

1. Why do Positivists believe that Sociology can be scientific?

2. Why do Interpretives believe sociology cannot be scientific?

3. Which argument do you find most convincing? Give reasons for your answer.

4. Why do Positivists prefer **Quantitative** data and Methods?

5. Why do Interpretive sociologists prefer **Qualitative** data and Methods?

Doing research

Learning objectives

1. Knowledge and understanding of the research process

2. Knowledge and understanding of key concepts and issues in the reserch process.

The questions sociologists ask are not so different from the questions we all ask at times – Is the family breaking down? Does the media encourage violence? In everyday life we answer these questions with reference to our families, friends and the media etc. These may be influenced by sociology but are often biased and limited. The sociologist tries to provide a more objective and accurate analysis. Good sociology is based on empirical evidence that has been produced by such methods. It is, as we previously mentioned, then published so it can be evaluated by others.

Sociological research is sometimes divided into three basic forms:

Descriptive – where the sociologist is seeking to gain information/knowledge, describe a social situation and perhaps make connections/correlations. For example 'How are the exam results of w/c and m/c pupils different?'

Explanatory – sociologists are not usually content with just describing a social phenomena, they want to explain it – to find the causes. In our example above they would want to find out 'Why the exam results of w/c and m/c pupils are different' (and ultimately why m/c pupils do better).

Action research – This is where the researcher is actively involved in planning/implementing some change in a particular social situation, and then in studying the effects of this change. For example a Sociologist may be involved in helping a school to introduce after school study sessions for disadvantaged (w/c) students. He would then study the effects of this change. Sometimes, however, sociologists may conduct an experiment without permission – remember Rosenthal and Jacobson's experiment on Teachers attitudes, labelling and SFP!

The stages of sociological research

Choosing a research topic

The Sociologist's choice of topic will be influenced by:

1. The **theoretical standpoint** and **values and beliefs** of the researcher. A Feminist, for example, is likely to focus on 'women's issues'. If studying education, she may well focus on gender issues - questions like 'Why girls are less likely to take science and maths at A-Level.' This raises possible issues of bias – will the values beliefs and interests of the researcher affect the objectivity of the research.

2.What is '**trendy and fashionable**'. The sociologist will be attracted to topics that are considered important at the time, by other sociologists, by the public, and by important groups like the Government.

3. **Sources of Funding** – Research cannot be done if you don't have the money! Those who provide research funds – Government, Business, Charities and Universities etc. may well want research done on certain topics that they are interested or that benefit them. For example the Government may want research done on the effects of its policies on education – the impact, for example, of schemes like 'Sure Start' on the performance of poor, w/c children. Again there are problems with this. Should sociologists research what Governments or Business think are important, or should they research what they think is important? (but of course they may not have the funds)

Reading around, Research questions and hypotheses

You have doubtless done many pieces of research in your educational life. When given a topic to research you would start by looking at what information is already available. This will help you to develop a research question or hypothesis.

1. **Research questions** are most usually used by those doing descriptive research, or by Interpretive sociologists. For example if you wanted to study the behaviour of an Anti-School subculture, you may well start with a general idea of trying to find out what their attitudes and values are – you may however, after some provisional research, develop a hypothesis.

. **Hypotheses are statements (not questions) that can be tested by collecting evidence**. They are preferred by sociologists who take a more 'scientific' approach. A hypothesis is a prediction about what the researcher will find out e.g. 'Teachers attitudes affect children's performance' (this was the general hypothesis tested by Rosenthal and Jacobson in their study of labelling and SFP – see education).

There are also **practical issues that influence both choice of topic and method – see below.**

Research design and choosing a method

Researchers have to decide whether to do primary research – i.e. use methods like observation or surveys to generate 'new' data; or to use information that already exists – secondary data, like government Statistics or previous research etc. Many other factors affect choice of methods – theory, ethical and practical issues. These will be dealt with in a later section of the module. Research design refers to the way in which the sociologist organises her research. Sometimes only one method will be used e.g. when **James Patrick** studied a Glasgow Gang (1970s) he used Participant Observation, just joining the group and taking part in their lifestyle. **Eileen Barker** however, in her case Study of a Religious Sect 'the Moonies', used a variety of methods and adopted a complex research design to test whether members had been 'brainwashed'.

Operationalising concepts

Whatever topic and method(s) a researcher chooses they will have to operationalise concepts. This requires defining a concept in terms that mean it can be identified and measured. For example in the field of education a researcher may want to find out why w/c children are more likely to 'fail' in education. But what does 'failure' mean, and how can it be measured? The researcher must therefore turn the vague concept of 'educational failure' into something more concrete. She may therefore decide to define educational failure as the failure to achieve 5 grade C or above GCSE grades. Now she can measure and compare w/c and m/c 'failure rates'. (but of course other researchers may disagree with this definition).

Gathering Data

Once the research design has been decided upon it can be implemented. The sociologist gathers their data. Often, particularly when using Questionnaires or interviews, a **pilot study** will be used to ensure the questions are not ambiguous and will be understood by the respondents.

Analysing and Interpreting results.

You must analyse your data and interpret it – apply it to your hypothesis. Does the evidence support your hypothesis (this requires interpretation of evidence). You would then need to write up a report of your findings (what have you found out?) and publish your report so that it can be evaluated by other sociologists

When there is strong evidence to support a hypothesis, and little to disprove it, we call it **a theory**.

A theory is a statement about the relationship between two variables (in sociology social phenomena or concepts) e.g. poverty causes educational failure. In sociological research it is rare to find a complete answer. Research and theories develop, old research is used as a basis for new.

Other important Stuff:

Causes and correlations

Sociologists are trying to find the **causes of social behaviour** – why do people commit crimes? Why do poor children do badly at school? To do this they look for **correlations (connections between variables/concepts/social phenomena)**. For example there is a close connection between social class and educational achievement. Researchers try to establish why social class affects success at school. But you have to be careful sometimes there may be a strong numerical connection between two variables yet the two are unrelated!

Social Problems and Sociological Problems

Social problems are 'problems and issues' in society – why people commit crimes, why people suffer from poverty, educational failure, inequalities of health etc. are all social problems, they are in addition **sociological problems**; topics that sociologists study and try to find causes of and possibly suggest answers to. **However sociological problems also include why people don't commit crimes, why people are wealthy etc. Sociologists are just as interested in explaining 'normal' behaviour as they are in explaining deviance and crime.**

Social Policy

Social policies are procedures and often laws that are introduced to solve social problems. These may be related to crime, education, health, the family etc. The idea is to support the social welfare of people in society. For example 'Sure Start' was brought in to help poor families and single parents with the care and education of their children. Pensions help the old etc. Sociological research can supply governments with evidence and theories that will help them decide on social policy. The government also commission/pay for research into social problems. Some sociologists are thus funded by the government. Others are critical of government funding, arguing that sociologists should be impartial and independent – research what they think is important.

Test your understanding

Using examples explain:

1. The difference between a social problem and a sociological problem.

2. The difference between a hypothesis and a theory.

Methods used in Sociological Research

Learning objectives

1. Knowledge and understanding of the use and application of different sociological methods, primary and secondary, quantitive and qualitative.

2. Evaluation of the strengths and weaknesses of different sociological methods.

3. Knowledge, understanding application/interpretation of sociological studies using different sociological methods.

Experiments

There are three basic types of experiments laboratory, field and natural experiments.

Laboratory experiments are done in controlled conditions, they are the classic method of natural science. **For example let's look at a classic experiment in biology – plant growth:**

Hypothesis : if you restrict a plants light you restrict its growth.

Method : take two very similar plants put one in light and the other in darkness. Keep all other variables constant e.g. moisture, heat, soil etc.

Measure plant growth. You can express the differences in quantitative form. Have you "proved" your hypothesis?

In this experiment light is the **independent variable** because it is the **causal factor**. Light is the **dependent variable** because it is the factor that is affected by the light.

In sociology, however things are much more complicated. Laboratory experiments are seldom used and even field experiments are not common. Natural experiments are very rare.

Lab experiments do have advantages:

1. They can produce numerical results to test hypothesis e.g. **Milgram's electric shock experiment** measured how far people were willing to go in giving people electric shocks (really no shocks were given – an actor pretended to suffer from the 'shocks'). The number of people who were willing and the level of shocks could be easily measured, to test the hypothesis that people are willing to obey people in authority – the "scientist". **Education link** – The subjects of the experiment were told that they were in an experiment to test the use of punishment in learning. This experiment relates to education because it shows peoples reactions to authority – obedience.

2. They can be **reliable** – i.e. if replicated they should give the same results.

3. They can be **objective**. The researcher may even hire others to carry out the research to avoid bias and remain detached.

However there are many problems with using Laboratory experiments in sociology

1. People are complex creatures they are not easy to experiment on because, unlike chemicals, plants and animals they are conscious beings who have choices in how they behave. So they **don't always react in predictable ways**

2. Because people are complex it is very hard to identify, let alone control, all the **variables** that may affect their behaviour.

3. An experiment is an artificial situation and, if people are aware of this, they may behave in an unnatural way. Therefore the method **lacks ecological validity**. For example the presence of the researcher may affect responses. The personal characteristics of the researcher –their age, sex, class etc may affect responses - we call this "**experimenter bias**" . In the Hawthorne experiment variables like heat and light were varied (in a factory). But however things were changed the output of the workers increased. It was concluded that it was the **presence of the researchers that changed peoples' behaviour** (called now the "**Hawthorne effect**").

4. Similarly people may behave in the way they think the researcher wants them to behave – we call these **demand characteristics**.

5. There are also **ethical considerations**. Is it right to experiment on people? Experiments may cause **physical or psychological harm**. **Zimbardo**, in his "prison experiment" got students to play the roles of prisoners and guards. The guards became cruel and oppressive the prisoner's victims, in the end the experiment had to be called off. People may be damaged by such experiments. Similarly in **Milgram's** experiment participants might have been psychologically damaged by the realisation that they had been prepared to give a person lethal electric shocks.

6. Sometimes researchers will deceive people about experiments so they don't know what's going on. This may make the experiment more valid but it is wrong to deceive people. Sociological research guidelines say that participants should give **informed consent,** except in exceptional circumstances.

7. Lab experiments are **rarely representative** – they are too small scale – 'you can't fit society into a Laboratory'.

Field experiments have the advantage of being more valid, because they are in "natural surroundings" but variables are even harder to control and again deception is often used. Such experiments are also often unreliable.

Education link

Rosenthal and Jacobsen did an experiment (Pygmallion in the classroom) to see the effects of teachers expectations on pupil performance. They gave pupils tests and told a teachers that the results of these tests showed that certain pupils were "spurters" i.e. pupils who would improve greatly over the next year. In fact the names were picked randomly. Sure enough they did improve because of the teachers attitude to them. However this experiment **involved deception** and it may have **damaged other pupils** who did not get the attention. Moreover when other researchers repeated it they did not get such strong results – i.e. it **was not reliable,** maybe because of the number of variables involved, that could not be controlled.

A final point. Interactionists sometimes use field experiments to test the meanings people give to situations. These involve qualitative data.

David Rosenhan 1973

In 1973 David Rosenhan got some of his students to pretend to be schizophrenic and had them admitted to psychiatric hospitals Once in hospital he had told them to act normally. not 'crazy in any way'. Interestingly they were all discharged (on average after 19 days) but with the schizophrenia 'in remission'. At no time in their stay was their illness questioned. In fact everything they did was seen as confirming their illness. If they protested that they were ok, it was seen as 'denial'. If they got angry it was seen as a 'symptom of their disease'. **Education link** – this shows again the impact of labelling. In schools as well teachers treat pupils according to their labels – not as individuals.

Natural Experiments

These are experiments where researcher do not attempt to control variables but observe some 'naturally' occurring situation/phenomena to see what the results are. Again this is rare in sociology and it is still very difficult to isolate the effects of one factor from other variables. A good example is sociological observation of **'Zero Tolerance' policing** in New York in the 90s. The New York mayor Rudy Giuliani introduced a policy of strict crackdowns on even petty crime. Zero tolerance policing means taking firm police action against all crimes, however small and so 'cleaning up neighbourhoods' and giving more major criminals 'no cover'. Sure enough crime rates fell significantly. However other research has pointed out that the 'zero tolerance' effect on serious crime is difficult to disentangle from other initiatives happening at around the same time in New York, for example 7,000 new policemen were 'put on the streets', social programs moved over 500,000 people into jobs from welfare at a time of economic buoyancy, and the supply of crack cocaine dropped in New York from 1990 to 1999. In addition the number of males aged 16-24 (the age group most likely to commit crimes) was dropping anyway due to demographic changes. This illustrates the difficulties of identifying the effects of one variable in natural experiments, when you cannot control others.

Test your knowledge and understanding

1. Explain what is meant by the concept of 'the Hawthorne effect'.

2. Explain what is meant by a field experiment.

3. Suggest two ethical problems in using experiments in sociological research.

4. Suggest two theoretical problems in using laboratory experiments in sociological research.

5. Examine the usefulness of different types of experiments in sociological research .

93

Asking Questions

One of the advantages that sociologists have over natural scientists is that they can ask the subjects of their research questions. Of course the disadvantage of this is that people can tell lies!

Social surveys

Social surveys involve the systematic collection and analysis of information from a certain population. This may be e.g. the population of Britain, or all males over 18, or divorced people living in Canterbury.

The methods used in surveys are usually structured questionnaires or structured interviews. They usually produce **quantitative** data and are thus **preferred by positivist/structuralist** sociologists. Surveys are not only used by sociologists they are used in market research and by the government. The Census (done every 10 years) is the biggest survey of all going to every household in the country. Government surveys like this provide very useful **secondary sources** for sociologists.

Sampling

Sociologists often need to study very large populations. It would be impossible, in terms of time and money, to question every person in Britain. Indeed even if the population being studied is only a few thousand a **sample** may have to be taken. A sample is a group which represents the social characteristics – age, sex, class, ethnicity etc. - of the group being studied. We call the group, that the sampling is taken from the **research population**. From this we get a **sampling frame** – a list of all the people in the research population. It is rarely easy to find or create a sampling frame of the group you are studying. If it is the adult population of Britain you could use the electoral roll, if students at your school, the school roll, but what if it is heroin addicts or single parents – where would you get that from?

Types of sample

Random – here the names are taken out of a hat – or today picked by a computer. This sampling is based on **probability**. Everyone has the same chance of being picked and so the sample is likely to be representative.

Stratified – here the sociologist **ensures all the important variables in the population are represented proportionally in the sample** – age, sex etc e.g. if the population you are studying is 70% female, your sample must be 70% female. In market research this is often done using quota sampling where interviewers are told to interview certain categories of people.

Random/stratified is a combination of the two types, it is used to ensure that small groups in your population are represented e.g. in a school there may be only 10 students doing A-level Physics. If we select just at random we may not get any of these students so we start by stratifying the sampling frame into subjects - Physics, English Sociology etc. then we randomly select the right number from each subject.

Snowball sampling/Opportunity sampling. This is where the researcher "**picks up" a sample as he/she goes along.** He may be introduced to other contacts by the people he is studying. This is unlikely to be representative but may be the only way of reaching people like criminals or drug addicts.

Selective or purposive sampling - here the sociologists **choose a group they judge to be appropriate**. This may be used to test a theory or other research e.g. Anne Oakley deliberately chose an unrepresentative sample to test Murdock's theory that all societies were characterised by male provider/female carer roles. By finding a few societies where this was not the case she disproved this general theory.

It is usually important that a sample is **representative** because if it is not then the results will not reflect the true behaviour/opinions of the group studied i.e. will not be **valid.** The sociologist therefore will not be able to make generalisations from the study. Some sociologists, however, may not be concerned with representativeness. Interactionist sociologists often study small groups and are concerned with understanding meanings rather than making generalisations and establishing "laws" of social behaviour.

Surveys can be 'Cross-sectional' – i.e. a 'snapshot' of people's attitudes/behaviour at a particular point in time or 'Longitudinal' i.e. the survey is repeated at set periods – often over a number of years.

Methods/Education link – a Cross-sectional survey – 'Boys and Girls 'Changing Attitudes'.

The research company **Kikland Rowell (2007)** conducted a **survey** to find out the attitudes of parents towards their children's education. The survey was in the form of a **Questionnaire**. It was sent to 500 secondary schools throughout Britain and was completed by 137,000 students and 280,000 parents – **a huge, and representative, sample**. Amongst its findings were that 67% of parents with daughters wanted them to go to university, compared to 62% of parents with sons. In addition 80% of girls wanted to go to university compared with 72% of boys. Whilst these differences may not be huge but they are of great significance in showing a fundamental change in attitudes from even 20 or 30 years ago, when it was considered far more important for sons to get qualifications.

This study illustrates some of the **advantages of using surveys/questionnaires in national, educational research**. There are millions of people involved in education, all over the country – parents, pupils and teachers. To achieve **representative** results (and so that you can **compare** the responses of different regions and make **generalisations)** you need a method that can reach a large, dispersed, population. Questionnaires such as this produce **quantitative data** and, even when done on this scale, can be quickly analysed using computer technology. We can produce clear, numerical results (as above) and it is likely to be **reliable** i.e. if repeated very similar results are likely to be achieved.

However the major weakness of this method is that the closed questions that must be used to get such statistical data mean that people are unable to expand their answers and show the meanings they attach to them – the reasons behind their responses - they **thus lack depth and detail** and, because respondents may have to 'choose a box to tick' means that they may be forced into an answer that is close but not exactly true. Results can therefore **lack validity**.

Cross-sectional surveys are amongst the cheapest and most time efficient forms of research, but they can only tell you what is happening at that exact moment in time – they can be quickly become out of date.

Note: For evaluation of surveys (cross-sectional) see also questionnaires and structured interviews. The same advantages and disadvantages and examples can be used in questions and essays.

Longitudinal studies are done over a period of time. The same sample is used and so **changes in behaviour and attitude can be identified and trends established.** They are usually done using surveys/questionnaires but Participant Observation and Case Studies are also often done over considerable periods of time. Examples include the Census, the BBC programme "7-Up" and the 'Child health and education survey' which has followed the progress of all children born between 3-9 March 1958 and produced fascinating information about the effects of things like divorce, class etc on peoples lives.

Advantages of a Longitudinal approach

---

1. The researcher can make comparisons over time. This approach allows us to identify trends and changes in behaviour.

2. Longitudinal **surveys** are **reliable** –the same questions are asked every time.

3. Same sample – means responses are less likely to be different because a different sample has been used.

4. Often **representative** because big samples are used.

Disagvantages

1. **Sample attrition** – people drop out, die, move or become unwilling to continue – this may mean the sample becomes **less representative.**

2. Similarly a sample such as the child health and education study would be overwhelmingly white (in 1958) now there are far more ethnic minorities in Britain so **it would not be representative of today.**

3. Knowing they are in a study may affect peoples responses, and so **lower validity**

4. **Time and cost** – can only be afforded by researchers with a lot of money (backing) and commitment.

5. Because they are mostly quantitative Longitudinal surveys lack validity, depth etc.

Education/Methods link – A Longitudinal Survey

Longitudinal Research by the **National Children's Bureau** (of all the children born in a single week in 1958) indicates that the brightest 20% did just as well whether they went to Grammar Schools or Comprehensives whilst children of lower ability did somewhat better at Comprehensives than at Secondary Modern Schools.

Longitudinal studies (usually in the form of surveys) are a method that has the ability to measure changes over time. We can identify the effects of variables like class, gender and family background on educational performance. For example the NCB survey found that children from single-parent backgrounds tended to achieve lower examination grades, and were more likely to leave school early. Surveys such as this have large samples and are likely to be **representative.**

However there is a big problem with **sample attrition** – people drop out and, in time this may make the sample **unrepresentative.** Also data collected tends to be quantitative and does not give us the reasons behind the statistics. Again if we take the NCB study, though it can tell us that children from single parent families tend to do badly in education, it cannot tell us why. Is it because of family structure – lack of a male role model, discipline and support? Or is it because such families often suffer from material deprivation because they are dependent on benefits?

Questionnaires

Questionnaires may be posted, handed out or put on the internet. They usually use **fixed response - closed questions** i.e. yes/no, or answer 'a b c or d' etc , but can use **open questions** – where the respondent writes in their own answer. They also often use **classification questions t**o determine people's age, sex etc so they can produce correlations.

Advantages

1. Questionnaires can be sent to a **large geographically dispersed sample** – all over Britain for example – especially postal and internet questionnaires.

2. **Large samples** can be obtained easily and quickly

3. If sampling is accurate results are likely to be **representative** and can be generalised

4. There is little or no face to face contact **removing any interviewer bia**s. This means people are more likely to answer honestly especially about personal matters - so greater validity.

5. Because the questions are pre-coded it is easy to present them in statistical form – also tables, charts etc. this makes comparison easy.

7. They are **reliable** i.e. the research can be replicated by others who should get the same/similar results i.e. can be verified or disproved.

8. Questionnaires are **one of the most ethical method**s. They are voluntary, therefore the sociologist can assume informed consent. They are also usually anonymous and confidential, so preserving privacy rights.

Disadvantages

1, Mailed and internet questionnaires give the researcher **no control** after they are sent out. This produces a number of problems:

2. **Low response rate** – 25% is considered good. This means that the sample may not be representative of those it was sent to. Certain types of people may be more likely to reply, those who have an interest in the topic, or those who have more time e.g. the retired, (a **self-selected sample**) so the results are **not representative**. This in turn means the sociologist cannot accurately generalise from the results.

3. Respondents may also **not understand the meanings of questions** – they may misinterpret them. There is no-one to explain questions to them. In effect therefore respondents may be answering different questions – so limiting the **validity** of the data.

5. Nor does the sociologist know if the intended person has filled it in – again **limiting validity**

6. Most questions are closed. Therefore only a limited response can be given – yes/no, a)b)c) this means the respondent cannot give the answer they want – none of the choices may be right – again **limiting validity.**

7. This also means answers lack depth and detail. The sociologist cannot probe for deeper meanings and feelings – so of limited use to **Interactionists.**

8. **Imposition** – in questionnaires and structured interviews the researcher is deciding the topics, questions etc. He is therefore imposing his view of what is important and relevant.

9. **Mailed/internet questionnaires** are often just ignored – people can't be bothered or do not see them as relevant – there also may be concerns about confidentiality on the net.

Open ended questions and the presence of researchers may overcome some of these problems – but create others –affecting responses (interviewer bias), and open ended questions are far harder to analyse and quantify and thus take far more time (and money).

A Pilot Study, carried out with a few respondents before the main study, can iron out problems such as ambiguous or misleading questions. Often **follow up interviews** with a small section of the sample may give greater depth as well as checking understanding. The most famous example of a survey in the form of a questionnaire is the **Census** which is sent to every household by government so it is **very representative**, can be generalised, and is **reliable, objective** detached etc. – *but* – people may lie (e.g. benefit fraudsters might not want government to know who is living in their house), also the homeless are left out, and despite fines many people, especially young males and migratory people, don't fill it in.

Eileen Barker used in depth questionnaires in her case study of **Moonies sect** – along with every other method under the sun! This gave her quantitative data so she could correlate membership of the sect with home background, age and gender. – but the questionnaire was very long and she only got a high response rate because they knew her.

Education/ methods link – Note this study also appears in the Education module

Smith and Tomlinson found that class was more important than race in explaining the underachievement of ethnic minorities. They found little evidence of racism in the results of the **Questionnaires** that they used. Ethnicity had little effect on performance, class was much more important.

Smith and Tomlinson took a **Positivist** approach. They used **questionnaires.** These provide a much more **representative** approach, as they could, potentially, be sent to thousands of students and teachers over a wide area. They would also probably be more **reliable**, if the sample used was **representative**. However a topic like racism is likely to produce **invalid** responses. It is a sensitive subject and teachers may not wish to appear racist. Therefore they may give **socially acceptable** answers. Furthermore if **closed questions** are used the researcher cannot probe for deeper meanings.

Test your knowledge and understanding

1. Explain what is meant by a 'Pilot Study'. (2 marks).

2. Explain what is meant by a cross sectional survey. (2 marks)

3. Suggest two ways in which sociologists can obtain representative samples (2 marks)

4. Suggest two problems in using longitudinal surveys in sociological research. (4 marks)

Structured Interviews

These are usually face to face or conducted over the telephone. They mostly use closed questions and have many of the advantages and problems of questionnaires. They do however have some other advantages and disadvantages:-

Advantages

1. Structured interviews have a higher response rate than Questionnaires- people are more likely to respond because of the personal touch. This means responses may be **more representative**.

2. The interviewer can explain questions – therefore answers are likely to be more accurate and **valid**

3. By **combining structured and unstructured questions** you can get more depth and allow respondents to qualify their answers, explain more fully, by using more open questions – more flexibility. When researchers adopt this approach we call it **'semi-structured interviews'**.

Disadvantages:-

1. **Greater cost and more time consuming** than Questionnaires often meaning **smaller samples**.

2. The characteristics of the interviewer – age, sex, race, looks etc. may affect the responses – **interviewer bias.**

3. Often the respondent may give the answers they think the interviewer wants – **demand characteristics**.

In both questionnaires and interviews questions must be carefully phrased so as to be understandable and unbiased. Leading questions and loaded phrases must be avoided.

The British Crime Survey is an example of a structured interview carried out on 40,000 people – every year to see what crimes they have suffered from. Structured interviews are often used in market research and opinion polls.

Dobash and Dobash used structured interview questions, in their study of battered wives, to get quantitative data about amount of assaults, regularity, injuries (along with unstructured interviews so that they could get greater depth and detail, and validity).

In fact sociologists often use a mixture of structured (closed) questions and unstructured (open) questions for exactly that reason. See the education link below.

Education/methods link - a semi-structured interview both these studies can also be found in the Education module

Carol Jackson (Lads and Ladettes in school 2006)

Jackson used **semi-structured interviews** in her research on 209 pupils in nine schools. It is not a large sample and could not claim to be representative, but it did enable Jackson to produce both quantitative and qualitative results and, by allowing pupils to **answer some questions 'in depth' and in their own words**, means that results were likely to be **valid**. However Jackson herself had some misgivings about whether she was asking **'leading questions'** and whether pupils were giving her the answers **they thought she wanted**. In addition when questioning pupils of this age it is more than likely that some will answer questions so as to 'seem cool' in front of the interviewer. Few 14 year-olds want to be seen as geeks.

> **Gerwitz, Ball and Bowe 1995,**
>
> **Used semi-structured interviews** to question parents about the way they made decisions over which schools to send their children to. They found that m/c parents were far more skilled in using the system for their children's benefit. They were more likely to use the appeals system, arrange interviews with heads and use contacts (Governors, teachers etc.) to ensure they got their first choice school. W/c parents tended to be 'disconnected choosers' they did not have the skills or knowledge to make informed choices or to use the system to their children's benefit.

Although structured interviews produce quantitative data there are a whole range of interviews which vary from the "highly structured questionnaire type" to 'unstructured interviews' which are more like conversations. Many come in between these extremes and may combine closed and open ended questions to produce "numbers and meanings" quantitative and qualitative data, as in the examples above.

Unstructured Interviews

Are favoured by **Interactionist** sociologists because they can reveal the meanings people attach to their behaviour and allow empathy and understanding.

> **Advantages**
>
> 1. High in **validity.** The relationship between interviewer and interviewee **rapport** may produce greater honesty, and the trust built up may allow questions on sensitive subjects.
>
> 2. Greater **depth and detail**
>
> 3. Respondents can answer in their own words – so give their **feelings and meaning**s how they want to.
>
> 4. **Flexibility**. The interviewer can follow up answers and go into different directions depending on what the interviewee says.
>
> 5. The interviewee has a lot of control so may be more comfortable, honest and co-operative.
>
> **Disadvantages**
>
> 1. Almost impossible to replicate and **unreliable** because every interview is, in a sense, unique.
>
> 2. **Time consuming and expensive** – both to do and to analyse results – hundreds of hours of tapes etc.
>
> 3. Results can't be made into statistics – can't establish trends etc.
>
> 4. Samples are small and **unrepresentative** – so can't generalise.
>
> 5. **Interviewer bias** – the social characteristics, or the rapport established may affect responses – respondents may "give the researcher what they think she wants to hear" or be negative.
>
> 6. **Imposition** – although the researcher does not "impose the questions" he/she does decide what to include and emphasise when the data is analysed and so may impose his/her interpretations. This imposition and **interviewer bias** may **reduce the validity** of the results.

Studies

Dobash and Dobash –used unstructured interviews to gain empathy and depth. It is much more appropriate for sensitive subjects and gave a real understanding of the suffering of battered wives. **Feminists, as well as Interactionists** like this approach – it allows women to "tell their own stories". It is a much more **valid** approach because there is less imposition and because of the **rapport** built up. But it took a great deal of time and money - interviews took up to 12 hours – so only a limited number of interviews can be carried out making the research **less representative or generalisable** - and it needs skilled interviewers. Rapport may cause **interviewer bias.**

Anne Oakley used unstructured interviews in her study of new mothers. As a mother herself she was able to empathise with the women and formed strong relationships with them. They felt comfortable and co-operated fully with her research – even becoming friends.

Paul Willis in his study of "the lads" in a secondary school, used Unstructured Interviews as part of his Observation. This allowed the lads to give their full views of school and life how they felt, and the meanings they attached to school; for example their dislike of authority and their rejection of academic knowledge. The lads could express their feelings in their own words thus gaining validity, empathy etc. But like all such studies it was based on a small sample and so was unrepresentative etc.

Note: Use the examples on semi-structured interviews when answering questions on unstructured interviews. Both studies contain unstructured 'questions'.

Guide to doing unstructured interview

1. Decide on your basic aims/research goals

2. Produce an interview schedule, defining the basic topics you want to discuss

3. Choose a comfortable setting where your interviewee will feel at ease

4. Try to establish trust and rapport through ordinary conversation

5. Guide the discussion towards your goal – but don't pressurise

6. Don't be afraid to go off at a tangent and follow up unexpected leads

7. Record your results during the interviewed – preferably electronically.

8. Analyse results.

Exercise: It is useful to compare different methods, this helps with the vital skill of evaluation. Draw out and fill in the table below:

	Structured Questionnaire	Structured Interviews	Unstructured Interviews
Validity			
Reliability			
Represent-ativeness			
Objectivity			

For each method write out whether it is high, low or medium for each 'concept'. Briefly explain why this is the case.

Group Interviews

Sometimes researchers may interview groups of people.

Advantages:

1. Uncover group dynamics and relationships.

2. They are a less formal situation so people may be more natural and relaxed – open up more.

3. More people can be interviewed in a shorter time.

4. People may be more comfortable with peers, so more honest (validity).

However

1. One or two people may dominate.

2. Some people may be reluctant to express themselves – or answer dishonestly, because of peer group pressure – problem with **validity.**

3. May go off the point.

4. Hard to record information – a lot of people talking at the same time

5. Most of the material gained from such interviews is again qualitative.

6. Hard to replicate – **unreliable.**

Test your knowledge and understanding

1. Explain what is meant by Interviewer bias.

2. Explain what is meant by socially desirable answers.

3. Suggest two practical problems associated with unstructured interviews.

4 Suggest two problems with using group interviews in sociological research.

5. Examine the usefulness of social different forms of interviews in sociological research on gender differences in education.

Watching and experiencing - Observation

There are a number of types of observation. **Most are qualitative but "structured observation" produces quantitative data.**

Structured observation

Here the researcher observes behaviour as an "outsider" she will have a tally chart of "behaviour" that she is looking for. She will mark down each type of behaviour as it occurs. For example, a researcher may go into a classroom to study the differences in behaviour between girls and boys. She may have "categories" like how often, and for how long, boys and girls talk, how much time the teacher gives to boys and girls etc.

Advantages

1. Produces **quantitative data** which can be expressed in numbers displayed as graphs and charts and used to test hypotheses.

2. Because the researcher is "**detached**" the research may be more objective because she is not involved.

3. **Reliable** – the observation can be replicated because the categories are the same. Thus another researcher is likely to get similar results.

Disadvantages

1. **Lack of validity** – will pupils behave in the same way if they know they are being observed? – **Hawthorne effect**

2. **Lack of depth and detail,** only quantitative results, no meanings or feelings. And **impossible to explore the reasons behind behaviour** e.g. why the teacher gives more time to boys.

3. **Lack of empathy** with pupils and teachers.

For these reasons **qualitative observation is more often use**d. This may be participant observation where the researcher actually joins in with the activities of the group or nonparticipant where the researcher remains an "outsider". Often sociologists, especially if studying deviant groups like drug addicts or racists will "semi-participate" whilst avoiding activities that may be harmful to herself or others.

Participant Observation

Advantages of participant observation

1. Empathy and understanding. You are part of the group, you can see things through their eyes.

2. Validity. Because the researcher is part of the group and can see their behaviour with his own eyes it is far harder to deceive him, so results are more true to life. Moreover you will be trusted so members are more likely to open up, and tell you the truth.

3. Depth and detail. You are with them everyday your depth of understanding is much better and you can record the rich detail of their lives.

4. You can study groups that would refuse to answer questionnaires and interviews – deviant groups like gangs and prostitutes.

5. You can observe **over time** so can see changes etc.

6. Flexibility. You are not imposing your views as you are in questionnaires. You can follow up leads and change course according to what you discover. **Whyte** said he "learned the answers to questions he would never have known to ask."

Disadvantages.

1. **Lack of objectivity** – you are so involved you may become biased. Some researchers have even "**gone native**" – joined the group they are studying.

2. The presence of the interviewer may affect the groups behaviour. Even in covert observation a new member will change the dynamics of the group (**Hawthorne Effect**) – means it is not as valid as some would claim.

3. **Can the observer really argue he understands the meanings the group give to behaviour** – its his interpretation – again a validity problem

4. You **cannot replicate**, each observation is unique and if you were to repeat it you would get different results – so **not reliable.**

102

5. **Small scale and not representative**. How can we be sure that, for example, the lads in the school that Willis observed are representative of those in other schools?

6. **Getting in -adopting a native costume.** You will have to fit in. If your sex, ethnicity, age etc don't match the groups you may be rejected or, at the least you are likely to affect behaviour –in covert observation you would not be accepted into the group.

7. In practical terms P.O. is **very time consuming and expensive**.

8. It is very difficult to **sustain a role** for a long period of time.

9. P.O. is also criticised for **focussing on powerless and deviant group**s – accused of "voyeurism" .

Non-participant observation has some advantages. Because the researcher is not involved he is **likely to be less biased** – more objective. Also, because he is not joining in, the group **may be less influenced by his behaviour.**
On the other hand it is precisely by becoming a member of a group that empathy is developed. There will be **less understanding and depth in the study**. It is also **easier for the group to hide behaviour**, and they may behave differently if they know they are being observed.

Public Domain Image.

Participant Observation was invented, almost by accident, by the great anthropologist Bronislaw Malinowski. During World War 1 he was in Samoa studying the Trobriand Islanders. Because he was an Austrian citizen he would have been arrested by the British. He was therefore stuck on the islands, living with the natives, and decided to study their lives in depth. No native costume though! That came later.

Covert and Overt Participant Observation

Both covert and overt methods have their own advantages, and problems. **Overt P.O.** is when the researcher informs the group of what he is doing he thus has **informed consent**. **Covert** is when the researcher infiltrates the group without their knowledge/permission.

Covert advantages

1. More **valid** because people behave more naturally if they do not know they are being observed.

2. Can access all areas of groups behaviour – known outsiders may be prevented from involvement in "secret areas"

3. Can dig deeper – using their status as a member.

4. **Greater empathy** – 'walking in other peoples shoes'.

Covert disadvantages

1. May be discovered which may destroy the whole research project.

2. Very difficult to record info – may have to rely on memory and write things down later which can lead to errors – **less validity.**

3. Ethical issues – no informed consent, deception, **possible damage to the group** on withdrawal.

4. Sociologists may have to engage in illegal/immoral activities or risk **blowing their cover.**

5. **Going Native** is more likely because of close involvement.

6. Getting in (how do you get access). **Staying in** (its hard to keep up pretence and sustain the role over time). **Getting out** (without damaging the group or endangering yourself – **see Patrick**)

Overt advantages.

1. Can **openly ask** questions (interview) to clarify meanings, without raising suspicion.

2. No deception, **informed consent** gained,

3. Don't have to join in all activities – if immoral or illegal

4. Members may **confide in you** as a trusted outsider – tell you things they would not tell a fellow member of the group.

Overt Disadvantages

1. The "**Hawthorne effect**" people may not behave naturally, if they know they are being observed. For example a deviant or criminal group may act less 'criminally' or alternatively more so to 'show off'.

2. The researcher may **not be allowed to witness some activities** – secret or deviant behaviour.

3. They may be **refused entry**. It is notoriously difficult for example to observe powerful groups like royalty or the Mafia!

Education/methods links

2. Paul Willis, Learning to Labour (1976) studied cultural reproduction in a boy's Secondary School. He found a strong conflict between the "Lads" (w/c, anti-school subculture) and the "lobes" (hard working pro-school pupils). The lads saw school as an alien and pointless institution

Willis adopted an "eclectic" approach combining a Marxist view with interpretive methods. He studied only one school and about a dozen 'lads'. This is therefore an example of a **case study.** Case studies often involve a variety of methods. Willis used **overt observation,** so the pupils knew he was studying them. This has many advantages; it means that the observer is being **ethical, because he has the consent of the subjects** of his research. It also means that he can **ask questions** (Willis also used **unstructured interviews**). Such **interpretive methods** allow the researcher to establish a bond with those they are studying and to uncover their '**motives and meanings'.** Because of this closeness the researcher can **empathise** – see the world through their subject's eyes**,** and this tends to produce **valid (true to life)** results. **Positivist** critics however would argue that such **a small sample cannot give representative results**, and that it is not **objective.** They would also argue that it is **not reliable** as it would be very unlikely that anyone repeating the research would get the **same** results. The 'lads' may have also 'played up' to Willis

104

and thus not behaved naturally – **the Hawthorne Effect.**

2. Cecille Wright (1986- 1992), used **observation** to study racism in both Primary and Secondary schools. She found that West Indian children are often labelled by teachers as disruptive and badly behaved. They were far more likely to be put in low streams and sets even when their ability matched that of white and Asian pupils in higher sets

3. David Gilbourns's research (1990) again using **ethnographic techniques - observation** and interviews with teachers and pupils - supports Wright. He found that although the vast majority of teachers try to treat all children fairly many had ethnocentric views regarding West Indian students as "trouble" so more were likely to be disciplined, reported, excluded than other pupils who committed similar offences etc.

Both Wright and Gilbourn used **ethnographic approaches** ,favoured by **Interactionist Sociologists,** by immersing themselves in the culture of the schools that they studied in order to achieve a more **valid** (true to life) picture. By actually observing the treatment of ethnic minorities you are less likely to be deceived. Ethnographic approaches are also more **empathetic** because the researcher is involved in the day to day culture of the school, they get to understand the meanings and feelings of the people concerned – both teachers and pupils. Though the subjects may 'put on an act' at first, if observed in an **overt (open) way** it is likely that in time they will behave normally, these methods achieve far greater **depth and detail**. Probing questions may be asked to clarify and deepen knowledge.

However the presence of the researcher may cause unnatural behaviour **(the Hawthorne effect)**. Teachers may, for example try to hide racist attitudes; black pupils may have been more, or less, disruptive. Such methods are also very dependent on the **interpretations** of the researcher. Other researchers may see the situation in a very different way. Thus these methods are **unreliable** (if repeated it is unlikely that they would get **the same results).** The small number of schools involved in both studies cannot possibly be seen as **representative** of the thousands of schools in Britain, therefore we cannot **generalise** these results.

Note all these studies are also dealt with in the Education section (above).
Participant observation – Studies and Exercise

Study the examples of observational research (below). For each example state:-

1. What kind of observation it is.

2. Why you think the researcher used observation of this type (advantages).

3. Problems/disadvantages - including ethical concerns.

a) A classic example of PO was **Whyte's study of Chicago gangs (1955)** He had an insider contact "Doc" and although others knew he was an outsider they did not know his exact purpose. Quotes from Whyte's study reveal some of the key advantages and disadvantages of the approach.

"I learnt the answers to questions I would not have known to ask"

"I got so involved I realised I was becoming a non-observing participant"

And Doc said "I began to realise that whatever I was doing I would be thinking about what William (Whyte) would think.

b) In the **1970s James Patrick studied a Glasgow gang**. He was a reform school teacher and was invited to observe by one of his "students" – the leader of the gang. Despite this he had problems in fitting in. He did the wrong button up on his jacket and, despite coming from Glasgow, found their accent very hard to understand. He also became involved in violence, drug taking and other illegal activities and although he took no part in violence (risking his cover!) he found the gangs violent criminality hard to handle and eventually left the gang. He published, under a false name, (obviously without permission) and had to leave Glasgow because of fears for his safety.

105

c)**Laud Humphreys (1971)** did his research on casual sex between men in public toilets. He was a lookout (watcher queen) and so did not actually take part in sexual acts whilst still gaining the trust of the men. Humphreys also noted the car registrations of the participants and was able to find their addresses and interview some. He found that many of the men were married and had "normal heterosexual sex lives". Many were, or had been, in the military.

d)**Eileen Barker** studied the "**Moonies**" a religious sect. She had to ask permission to get access. This took two years. A further 6 years were spent studying the group. Besides observation Barker used interviews and questionnaires as well as secondary sources. - a classic example of methodological pluralism. Obviously Barker faced the problem of validity – would members behave in the same way if they knew she was observing? (Hawthorne effect) but she found that in time people did not "put on an act" indeed it had advantages, they would confide in her because she was not an actual member of the sect. Her approach also avoided ethical problems.

e) **Phillipe Bourgois (In Search of Respect !990s) studied 'crack dealers' in East Harlem**, New York. The dealers knew he was writing a book, and were more than pleased to be in it 'I deserve a chapter Phillipe' so there was no problem with informed consent. The dealers: Primo, Caesar etc told Bourgois everything about their lives – the violence, the murders, the gang rapes, at times he was appalled and found it very hard to continue the study. Nor did he tell the police about offences they committed. Bourgois produced an in-depth study, that he could not have achieved in any other way.

Test your knowledge and understanding

1. Explain what is meant by Structured Observation.

2. Explain what is meant by 'a native costume'.

3. Suggest two ethical problems associated with Covert Observation.

4. Suggest two advantages in using Overt Observation in sociological research.

5. Evaluate the strengths of different forms of observation in Sociological research.

Secondary Sources

Primary data is collected first hand by the sociologist. The data does not exist before the research. In many ways the use of primary methods is preferable to the use of secondary. There are a number of distinct **advantages:**

1. The data is **specific to the research aims**- what you find out is all directly relevant.

2. The researcher is **in control** – she decides on the best methods to use – what questions are asked, when and with whom the observation takes place etc. – she decides if qualitative or quantitative methods are better.

3. The researcher **controls the research sample**, so knows how **representative** it is.

4. Sometimes no secondary data exists.

5. Material will be **up to date** as well as clearly focusing on the research aims.

However there are disadvantages:

1. Primary methods are often time **consuming and expensive**.

2. So there is the **problem of getting funding**, and who you get it from may influence your research and what methods you choose.

3. Primary methods often have **ethical problems** because you are directly **imposing on people**, and may **compromise their privacy, or harm them** in some way.

4. Plus all primary methods have their own distinct disadvantages (see above)

Secondary sources are sources that already exist. There is a huge amount of data 'out there' that can be useful to the sociologist – in books and articles, in the media and on the Internet. Secondary sources include Official Statistics, historical sources, personal documents like diaries and letters and life histories, and the mass media and Internet, which provide a huge and ever growing source of materials for Sociologists to study.

Using Secondary sources has numerous advantages:

1. The use of Secondary sources **saves time and often money** – why create new data if it already exists and is easily available?

2. If the research has a **historical dimension** it is often the only method available. If for example you want to study changes in education over the past 150 years you will have to use secondary sources. Nobody is left alive who went to school 150 years ago!

3. Secondary materials may also be used to **check a Sociologists findings. (Triangulation)**

4. Existing research is often used by Sociologists **to give background information** and to **help them form their hypotheses and/or research questions.**

5. The problems of validity and reliability can often be overcome by using a variety of sources so you can then **"cross-check"**

6. Often the material is **pre-analysed so it is easy to use.**

7. Some sources, like Official Statistics have **large and representative samples and tend to be reliable.**

Problems with using Secondary sources revolve around questions of authenticity, availability, validity and bias.

1. **How do we know if the source is authentic?** It could be a **forgery,** a famous example of such a forgery were the 'Hitler Diaries'. These were accepted by many experts, published in reputable newspapers but were later found to be fakes!

2. Obviously if the information is not available it cannot be used.

3. The focus of the study, and the methods used, **cannot be controlled** by the sociologist, because the research has already been done!

4. Information is often patchy and incomplete.

5. Other people have produced, collected and interpreted it. **How do we know if the methods were reliable and the interpretation valid?**

6. **Qualitative** sources are very **unlikely to be representative or reliable.**

7. **Quantitative** sources like official statistics may not **be valid.**

Even when secondary sources are available we must question their usefulness and accuracy? We must ask
1. **What methods were used to obtain it?**
2. **Who compiled it, and for what purpose?**
It may be that the author of such materials was giving a personal or biased view, that he lacked adequate information. or was simply lying.

Education/methods link. Research study (Lisa Harker 2006)

Harker produced a report for the Housing Charity Shelter, in which she reviewed a range of available evidence **i.e. she used Secondary Sources** –studies made by other sociologists she identified a number of negative effects that poverty may have on children's educational performance:

Harker used **Secondary sources** in her research. Such an approach saves both time and money as in this case such sources are readily available. It would also have enabled her to produce a far more wide-ranging report than she would have been able to using **primary research.** She could

107

also have compared research to test its **reliability** (reliability in sociology refers to whether research can be repeated and produce 'the same' results). In this case Harker would have been examining whether the research she looked at gave similar results.

There are however problems in using secondary sources:

Because you haven't done the research yourself you don't have any **control** over the methods used, so it hard to say how **valid** (accurate/true to life) it is.

Similarly there may also be **bias.** Researchers may have been committed to the idea of educational equality and perhaps 'found what they were looking for'.

Harker herself was **working for Shelter** , a charity for the homeless, therefore she might have tended to be **selective** i.e. using the material which backed the views of the charity.

This study also features in the Education module.

Quantitative secondary sources

Official Statistics refers to information which comes from the Government - the most famous example is the **Census** which is sent to every household every ten years. This must be filled in, by law and deals with questions like family structure, transport, occupation, and leisure. Other examples include the **General Household Survey, School League tables** and the **British Crime Survey.** Other Official Statistics include **Crime Statistics**, **Employment statistics**, and thousands of other "facts and figures" both from the Government and other groups like **Charities** and **Pressure Groups**.

These statistics are of immense value to sociologists:

Advantages

1. They are readily available and often free! **So save time and money.**

2. **Sample sizes are often very large** and as such surveys are done by qualified people they are likely to be **representative** and **reliable.**

3. **Hard Statistics** -Many Government statistics are "hard" and I don't mean difficult to understand! Hard Statistics are, unusually, **both reliable and valid** – they accurately measure what they are supposed to and if someone checks the data they will get the same results. **Marriages, divorces, births and deaths are examples of hard statistics**. They may be the odd unknown about death or birth but these are few and far between.

4. Many surveys are carried out on a monthly, yearly or ten yearly basis. They thus allow the sociologist to **compare over time and identify trends.**

. **Disadvantages**

1. **Soft Statistics** are much more problematic than hard statistics. This is because **what they measure is harder to define and much less clear-cut. Police crime figures** only measure the amount of crimes reported to and recorded by the police – a small minority of crimes. Even the **British Crime Survey** relies on peoples memories and cannot measure "victimless crimes" and those that are undiscovered – like fraud etc. Similarly suicide statistics depend on Coroners decisions and it has been found that Coroners have different criteria for defining Suicide. In Catholic countries for example Coroners are far less likely to give suicide verdicts.

2. Official Statistics are **Government statistics and may be politically biased**. The Conservative government of the 1980s and 90s changed the way unemployment was defined and counted over 20 times – every change but one resulted in a decrease in unemployment numbers!

3. **Marxists** would argue that statistics that are published by the government are intrinsically biased. They present information processed and produced by a Capitalist State to support the Capitalist system.

4. Interactionists would argue that official statistics **only represent how the "Authorities" define things like suicide and crime** e.g. Suicide isn't an objective measure of how many suicides there are but a measure of how many deaths Coroners have defined as suicide. It, like crime statistics, is thus **socially constructed.**

5. Other Statistics can also be questioned. Groups like Shelter, the N.S.P.C.C. etc have a vested interest in presenting information to support their cause.

The Census

The Census is generally regarded as the **most reliable and representativ**e of all Government "official statistics". It is sent to every household and has to be completed by law. The information it provides is essential for Government planning - how many schools, roads, hospitals etc. will be needed etc. So it is with some embarrassment that the government has had to admit that in two recent censuses (1991 and 2001) they have "mislaid" about 700,000 young men, many of these have gone to live abroad, or are living with single mums who don't want to lose their benefits.

Methods Education link.

School League tables are said to show which schools are the best, by publishing their A-Level, GCSE and SATS results. Such results are **representative** – they cover every school in the country. They are **reliable,** if you could replicate the research you would get the same statistics. Using these statistics would also save a lot of time and money. However, in actual fact League Tables only show which schools get the best exam results. Many schools get rid of unwanted students (who won't get good results) and anyway results mostly depend on intake. Selective schools and those with middle class pupils are bound to do better. In addition many schools switched to 'vocational GCSEs' to improve their results – these are supposed to be the equivalent of 4 GCSEs- but critics argue they are much easier. So it can be argued that the league tables are not **valid.**

The Learning and Skills Council (LSC) (a governmental body with the purpose of funding and promoting further education) produced a large scale survey of more than 2,000 adults and found that 27% regretted not making the most of the opportunities at school. More than one in four (30%) of those who had completed retraining said it had made them more employable and 17% had got a pay rise. The LSC interprets these statistics as showing the benefits of re-training. The study is again reliable and representative and yet if we look at them another way:

70% of respondents had found that retraining had had no effect on their employability and 87% did not get a pay rise!

In other words the LSC is putting a 'spin' on the results – to support their work and the policies of the government.

Qualitative Secondary data
Personal Documents
There is a huge range of qualitative secondary data available to Sociologists – novels, media sources (TV, newspaper, internet etc,), photographs and personal documents. In fact any 'cultural product', can be a useful source for research - from music to clothing to toys.

Personal documents. Examples of personal documents include informal life histories, diaries and letters. These tend to be **valid** and honest, because they are personal and not usually produced with the intention of publishing them, so people write their feelings down in an honest way. Diaries etc can also allow us to develop **empathy** for the people we study and they are written in the authors own words and so give their 'meanings and feelings' about their lives. They can provide richness and depth to a Sociological study.

Personal documents, however, are written from one persons point of view and so may be **biased** or misleading. People often try to present themselves in a positive light. Some personal documents may be produced with the intention of future publication e.g. politician's diaries, so are likely to present the politician, and their ideas, in a favourable light. Because such documents are personal they are **not representative** and of course you cannot repeat, or often check them, they are thus unreliable. In addition, as we have seen, such documents may be forgeries.

Willmott and Young used informal life histories and diaries in their study of family life in Bethnal Green.

Other qualitative sources – may include pictures, the media, novels etc etc. (see below – historical sources and content analysis)

Documents can provide a great deal of information about research subjects. Bank statements and bills can tell us about standards of living and patterns of consumption, whilst photograph albums and diaries can give us more qualitative, meaningful data.

Content Analysis

Some Media material is based on current research on a large scale and provides up to date information for Sociologists. Current Affairs and Documentary programmes are particularly useful. One must remember however that the sociologist must check the accuracy of such material, it may be politically or otherwise biased.

More often Sociologists use the media critically in the form of **content analysis.** This can be applied to T.V. Radio, newspapers, magazines, posters etc. The most famous exponents of this are the **Glasgow Media Group** who have used the technique to show political bias in the media (as well as sexism and racism) Such analysis could, for example, examine the roles played by black people in T.V. drama to see whether stereotypes are commonly used. It can examine the use of language and images.

Content analysis can be both quantitative and qualitative. Researchers can, for example, count the number of times disabled people appear in quiz shows and see how this compares to the number of people in society who are disabled. It can also be qualitative, e.g. analysing the way gender is represented in children's books.

Public Domain Image. Content Analysis.

Gender bias exists in the content, language and illustrations of a large number of children's books **(Jett-Simpso n & Masland, 1993)**. This bias may be seen in the extent to which a gender is represented as the main character in children's books and how that gender is depicted. Numerous studies analysing children's literature find the majority of books dominated by male figures. For example **Ernst (1995)** did an analysis of titles of children's books and found male names represented nearly twice as often as female names. She also found that even books with female or gender-neutral names in their titles in fact,frequently revolve around a male character. Many classics and popular stories where girls are portrayed usually reflect stereotypes of masculine and feminine roles.

Methods/Education link

Children's books frequently portray girls as acted upon rather than active **(Fox, 1993)**. Girls are represented as sweet, naive, conforming, and dependent, while boys are typically described as strong, adventurous, independent, and capable **(Ernst, 1995; Jett-Simpson & Masland, 1993)**. Boys tend to have roles as fighters, adventurers and rescuers, while girls in their passive role tend to be caretakers, mothers, princesses in need of rescuing, and characters that support the male figure **(Temple, 1993)**. Often girl characters achieve their goals because others help them, whereas boys do so because they demonstrate ingenuity and/or perseverance. If females are initially represented as active and assertive, they are often portrayed in a passive light toward the end of the story. Girl characters who retain their active qualities are clearly the exception **(Rudman, 1995)**. Thus, studies indicate that not only are girls portrayed less often than boys in children's books, but both genders are frequently presented in stereotypical terms as well.

Exercise – Think of stories you know – fairy tales, children's novels etc. Do they seem sexist to you? You might try a bit of your own content analysis of magazines, textbooks etc. to see if they present stereotypical images of gender and/or ethnicity.

Historical sources can be both qualitative and quantitative They are vital to Sociologists in establishing patterns of social change. **Weber** relied on such information in his classic work **"The Protestant Ethic.** Another example was the work of **Peter Laslett** who, using statistics from Parish Records, exploded the myth of the dominance of the extended family form in pre-industrial Britain.

Philip Aires used qualitative sources such as portrait paintings to argue that childhood was not accorded a special status in Medieval times. Aires also used written sources to corroborate this evidence.

Qualitative sources like novels newspaper articles etc may also allow the sociologist to gain a greater understanding of, and **empathy** for, the people and the times.

We do however have to be careful about the **validity** of such sources. Are they authentic? Is the author telling the truth or is the document biased? History tends to be written by the winners and by those who can write! (the higher social classes) so there is inevitable bias. A variety of sources should be used to check for validity, though sometimes few sources exist.

Public Domain Image
Historical documents can be vital in studying social change.

The Comparative Method

This was the classic method used by all the founding fathers of Sociology. It was seen as the **best alternative to experiments.** In this method the researcher uses existing information in the form of historical documents, statistics and records etc. to compare one society (or elements in it) with another.

The researcher:-

1. Gathers the relevant information
2. Compares this for different societies
3. Tries to identify the independent variables that explain a particular social fact.

This was the method used by **Weber in the "Protestant Ethic".** He was examining why Capitalism developed in Europe rather than China or India which had a similar level of technological and industrial development. He identified the Protestant (Calvinist) Religion as the independent variable which led to Capitalist activities.

Similarly **Durkheim in his study of suicide** found that some societies had higher rates of suicide than others. He identified the factors that accounted for this (he found that the unmarried, childless, protestant, urban dwellers etc had higher rates) and concluded that lack of integration caused higher suicide rates. Thus suicide was a social fact and not just an individual action.

Test your understanding

1. Read through the information. List all the sources mentioned under the headings Qualitative or Quantitative.
2. What are the 3 main general advantages and disadvantages of using secondary sources?
3. a) What advantages are there, for the Sociologist, in using Official Statistics?
b) Using examples, illustrate the problems involved with using Official Statistics.
4. Why should the information produced by Pressure Groups be questioned.
What considerations should be taken into account when using historical sources?
112

6. Which do you think would be a more valid account of a political meeting, the official report or a politicians diary? Explain your answer.

7. a) Why is the comparative method compared to an experiment?

b) Why is it less reliable than the experimental method?

8. How would Durkheim's research be criticised by Interactionists?

9. What are the main advantages of using Qualitative secondary sources like novels and personal documents? What are the limitations of such sources?

Other methods

Life histories

These are usually done using unstructured interviews although sometimes secondary sources are also used. Their aim is to provide an in depth picture of an individual and their lives to provide a personal history of changes.

The study of "**John Stands in Timber" a Native American, by Margot Liberty** is a famous example of a **Life History**. At first she tried to 'get information out of her subject', but quickly realised this was not an effective method. She then switched to 'unstructured, conversational' interviews in which John could say what he wanted to say. John Stands in Timber was one of the few Cheyenne who could remember the 'old days' of the Indian Wars and Margot Liberty obtained a **wealth of detailed, in depth information that she could not have obtained in any other way**. Of course there are problems with this kind of research. Other Cheyenne argued that Stands in Timber was **biased** in favour of the Crow Indians – a traditional enemy. Life histories are **time consuming and not representative**, they are just one persons view, and they **lack reliability** – they are very hard to replicate, though they **can be checked against other sources** – many Anthropologists had produced accounts of Cheyenne life in the 19th century. There are also questions about validity. Whilst Life histories give us a **deep and empathetic account** of people from the subjects point of view, they are **reliant on memory**. Stands in Timber was very old when he was interviewed and was trying to recall a period of seventy years of his life.

Methods/education link. Ethnographers also use the method of Life histories., which they 'build up' over time to produce in depth accounts of their subjects. **Phillipe Bourgois (In Search of Respect)** built up life histories of his informants – including Primo and Caesar, two 'crack dealers'. In one part of his study Bourgois explored Primo's school experiences. We learned that Primo had been immediately labelled as the 'ignorant and stupid son of an immigrant who did not even speak English'. When reading Primo's account we can understand the fear and inadequacy he felt in his first days at school and begin to understand why he became abusive. He recalls at the age of six shouting at his teacher 'Shut your mouth you f...... whore'.

This account provides us with an empathetic and rich understanding of the effects of labelling and SFP on one individual – it also links to Willis' study of the 'lads'. However it may well be that Primo exaggerates his behaviour, to show off to Bourgois and Caesar. One of the problems with Life histories is that people often tend to depict themselves in a more sympathetic or 'exciting' way.

Note – you can use both these studies when assessing both Unstructured interviews and Case Studies.

Advantages and disadvantages of life histories - Summary

1. Such studies are often **strong on depth and detail** as well as empathy – they tend to be qualitative using unstructured interviews or personal documents – allowing the subject to **speak for themselves** and thus, it is claimed are **valid.**

2. They also show **changes over time** – development.

113

> **Disadvantages**
> 1. They are often **not replicable or reliable.**
> 2. They often **rely on memory so may lack validity**.
> 3. **Not representative** – are only one (or a few) persons point of view.

Case studies

These are **"in-depth studies" of a person or group – of one good example**. Many studies are , in a sense, case studies – Willis study of "The Lads", the study of "John Stands in Timber", Eileen Barkers 'Moonies', Bourgois 'Crack Dealers'. They often use a variety of methods and sources. Barker, for example, used Overt Observation, questionnaires, interviews and secondary sources. They are thus an example of **Methodological Pluralism** – the use of a range of methods to produce an in-depth picture. They also enable you to. cross check one method with another to assess accuracy –**Triangulation**. The big problem lies in finding a typical example. What is true for one school or family may not be true for another – thus results are **unlikely to be representative** and this means you cannot generalise them to the whole population.

> **Test your knowledge and understanding**
>
> 1. Explain what is meant by life histories .
>
> 2. Explain what is meant by a case study.
>
> 3. Suggest one advantage and one disadvantage associated with case studies.
>
> 4. Suggest two advantages in using Life histories in sociological research.
>
> 5. Suggest two problems with using Life histories in sociological research.

Choosing a method

In the 'Doing Research' section of this module we briefly looked at choice of method. In this section we will examine these influences in more detail.

Theory plays a major part in deciding what methods to employ. As we have seen **Positivists** prefer to use methods like surveys that produce quantitative data that can measured, put into numbers and used to test hypotheses. **Interactionists,** on the other hand, are concerned with finding people's 'feelings and meanings', and tend to use qualitative research like participant observation and unstructured interviews. **Feminists also favour qualitative methods**. They argue that "scientific" sociology is patriarchal. It ignores the feelings and meanings which women emphasise. Women must be allowed to tell their own stories, the way they want to, through unstructured interviews etc.

Ethical issues Any form of research is, in some way interfering with peoples lives. Social sciences all have "ethical codes" which try to limit any damage. Key issues:

> **1. Confidentiality**. Will people reading the research be able to identify who took part? Even if they have agreed to do the research participants have a right to be anonymous if they so wish. This is more of a problem in P.O. or unstructured interviews which are in depth and involve small groups than questionnaires which are large scale and often anonymous anyway.
>
> **2. Consent.** Researchers should have **informed consent** from participants. They should know they are involved in research and the purpose of it. People have the right to privacy. However in some research – P.O. some experiments etc. if people know they are being researched they behave differently –the Hawthorne effect. The issue then becomes one of 'the right to privacy v the publics 'right to know'.
>
> 3. As we have seen some **methods like Experiments and Participant Observation have more ethical issues than others**. In Covert P.O. the researcher may have to be involved in illegal or

114

immoral behaviour or risk blowing their cover. Subjects of experiments may be upset or damaged by their experiences (see above for examples) and in any form of P.O. (and in unstructured interviews) the researcher gets close to the respondent and may cause damage when he withdraws from the research. The results of questionnaires may be used in
controversial ways.

Practical issues -A number of practical and personal issues will affect the methods researchers use:

1. Cost and time – some methods are far more time consuming and costly than others. Whereas postal questionnaires are a relatively quick and cheap method of research Longitudinal studies and Participant Observation methods take a long time – months and years, and so need generous funding sources.

2. Funding - Government and other agencies who finance research often want quick and "scientific" results so prefer surveys in the form of structured interviews or questionnaires.

4. The nature of the group. Large and geographically dispersed groups will need postal questionnaires. Small and secretive groups may need covert P.O. (they would be reluctant to co-operate with other research).

5. The characteristics of the researcher. A 'native costume' is required to do covert P.O. – the researcher must be able to fit in. Also the age, sex, ethnicity of the researcher can affect the interview process (interviewer bias).

6. The skills personality and circumstances of the researcher are important. Covert P.O can be dangerous and involve long periods away from ones family. Keeping up an act is difficult, and may put great psychological strain on the researcher. Unstructured interviews require great skill and patience etc etc.

7. Access and opportunity – Some Methods, particularly P.O. are often only possible with contacts - James Patrick could not have taken part in the Glasgow gang if he had not been a teacher at the reform school that the leader of the gang went to.

A final note. Researchers often use a variety of methods so that the strengths of one can compensate for the weaknesses of others. And remember that although all these factors are important theoretical issues involve a positive choice to take a certain approach whereas practical and ethical issues are constraints.

Test your knowledge and understanding

1. Explain what is meant by positivism.

2. Explain what is meant by qualitative methods.

3. Suggest two practical factors that might influence a sociologists choice of research method.

4. Suggest two ethical factors that might influence a sociologists choice of research method.

5. Evaluate the importance of ethical factors in a sociologists choice of research methods.

AS and A-Level exam type questions and tips

Methods questions are to be found on AS Paper 2 (Research Methods and Topics in Sociology) and A-Level Paper 1 (Crime and Deviance with Theory and Methods).

On the AS paper Q1 is a short answer question, worth 4 marks. You will be asked to outline two points, so only short explanations are required.

Give a clear answer and, if you are not completely sure, try to give an example so that you may, at least, gain one mark.

.You may be asked to identify advantages and/or problems of using a a particular method in sociological research e.g.

1. 'Outline two problems of using postal questionnaires in sociological research.'
2. 'Outline two advantages/strengths of using unstructured interviews in sociological research.'
3. 'Suggest one advantage and one problem in using official statistics in sociological research.'
Practice doing variations of these questions using different methods and be careful in the exam, for example, not to give advantages when problems are asked for! This may seem blindingly obvious but you would be amazed at how many students do it!

Remember **PET,** unless specifically asked for one type problems and strengths can be practical, ethical or theoretical (concepts).

Explain your answer briefly. Don't just put things like 'expensive' or 'valid', briefly explain why.

For Q1, for example, one of your answers might be *'Questionnaires may not be representative because there is often a low response rate and only a certain kind of person may (perhaps one interested in the subject) send them back"*
You would probably get 2 marks for the answer but it's worth making sure.

Similarly for Q2 **'One Strength of Unstructured interviews is that rapport may be built up and so people are more willing to open up and give more valid answers.**

Q2 on the AS paper is an essay question worth 16 marks.

It is an 'Evaluate' question. Usually the question will focus on the **strengths or weaknesses** of a method, if it does this don't do a simple advantages followed by disadvantages answer – focus on what the question tells you to, with **point by point evaluation.**

Examples of methods essays:

1. 'Evaluate the problems of using participant observation in sociological research.' (16 marks)

2. 'Evaluate the advantages/strengths of using unstructured interviews in sociological research.' (16 marks)

Look at the following example (Q2) of how to evaluate a point in this type of essay:

'One of the great advantages of unstructured interviews is that the interviewer can build a rapport with the interviewee and this leads to greater trust and honesty in responses, thus producing greater validity. However this can also have its problems. If the two become too close the 'interviewer effect' may take effect and the interviewee may give answers that he/she hopes will please the researcher and aid their research.............'
116

Another example (Q1)

One of the ethical problems in using covert participant observation is the lack of informed consent. Because the subjects of the study are being observed secretly they are obviously unable to give their permission. The researcher is in effect deceiving them by pretending to be a member of the group and yet it is precisely this act of deception that gives covert participant observation one of its great advantages as a method. Because they do not know they are being observed the research subjects are likely to behave naturally and thus the results of the research will be more true to life – ecologically valid........

Note how in these examples the evaluation points are directly related to the advantage/problem given. This is what you need to practice for this essay.

'Examine the usefulness of using postal questionnaires in sociological research'. (20 marks)

In the A-Level exam the only 'pure' methods question is Q5 on paper 3. Though there is also a theory and methods question and a methods in context question – see below.

Examples of A-Level methods question:

1. Outline and explain two advantages of using official statistics in sociological research. (10 marks)

2. Outline and explain two problems in using life histories in sociological research. (10 marks)

AS with other 10 mark questions on the A-Level paper you need to explain your two points in some depth. Again remember **PET**, advantages and problems can be ethical, practical or theoretical (concepts).

Here is an example of what is required for one advantage in Q1:

'One advantage of using official statistics is that they are usually representative. This is because they are produced on behalf of the government, often at considerable expense, and often involve huge samples. In some cases e.g. the Census it is a a legal requirement to complete the questionnaire. Therefore the material gathered will represent the views of the research population. However even the Census is not fully representative. Some groups, such as the homeless and migratory workers, are left out because they have no address to send the forms to!'

Note the use of a concept here, the full explanation of why official statistics are likely to be representative (with an example) and a little bit of evaluation.

Here is an example answer for Q2:

'One of the biggest problems with life histories, such as Margot Liberty's study of 'John Stands in Timber' is that they rely on the accuracy of the memory of the interviewee, often over a whole lifetime. People forget or may remember things in distorted ways, hence the validity of the material may be questioned. In this study, example other members of the Cheyenne tribe felt that John Stand in Tiber's account presented the Crow in a too positive light. There may be no other way of checking the validity of account – especially if there are no other survivors, though other accounts written at the time may be used to compare with the life history.

The Methods in Context Question.

This question is, in some ways, different from any other essay questions on both AS and A-Level papers. It requires you to **apply your knowledge and understanding of methods** to the study of a particular issue in education, and to evaluate the method in question. The methods in context question is to be **found** on Paper 1 of both the AS and A-Level Exam.
In this question you will be given an item, this is important, as it will provide some material that you can develop (not just copy!) in your answer, but you will also need to use your own knowledge of research methods and apply this to the topic in question.

Look at the following examples which apply to **both** the AS and A-Level exam:

1. Applying material (from the item) and your knowledge of research methods, evaluate the strengths and limitations of using unstructured interviews to investigate streaming.

2. Applying material (from the item) and your knowledge of research methods, evaluate the strengths and limitations of using self-completion questionnaires to investigate unauthorised absences from school.

How to maximise your marks
There are basically 3 mark levels:
1. If you just write about the advantages and disadvantages of the method in question – without relating it to education you can only get a maximum of 11/12 marks – and to get these marks you will need to use theory, concepts and ethics in some detail
2. If you relate the method to education in general you can get up to 14 marks.
3. If you relate the method to the specific research issue in question you can get up to 20 marks.

Level 1 marks
Here you need to identify and explain the general advantages of the method in question. For example for Q2:
'*Self-completion questionnaires are confidential and can be completed in private, therefore pupils or parents may be more honest about their behaviour and so results will be more valid*'

This is clearly just a methods point there is no reference to education or the topic involved.

Obviously we want to get into the top two mark levels.
    Level 2 marks
To get these marks you need to concentrate on **the research subjects** i.e. the people and groups/institutions you will need to research:
- pupils
- parents
- teachers
- the educational system (schools, government etc).

And examine the **practical, ethical and theoretical** (+concepts) issues (**P.E.T.**) of the particular method you are examining in your answer.
So what are these issues?
They include:
Access to children, teachers, parents and schools.
The **social characteristics** of the research subjects – their age, sex, ethnicity etc.
The **nature of schools** as institutions.

Access issues apply to all methods. There are many **gatekeepers** in education – headteachers, governors, teachers, parents, who may refuse you access. The school and teachers may also be suspicious of an outsider studying them and refuse permission (especially if they think the research may damage the image of the school (e.g. Research on sexism, racism, anti-school subcultures, labelling etc). If researchers need to enter the school they will also **need a CRB check.**

This is therefore a **big disadvantage/problem** for methods like Observation, P.O. Interviews (of all types), experiments, school documents etc, in fact all methods where you actually need to go into a school. But it is an advantage for methods like using Official Statistics, or questionnaires because you don't necessarily have to go into a school.

Lets take an example.
'In order to do research into education you need to study children. This raises ethical issues – children are under 18 and so you need parental permission to interview/question etc. them. There is also the question of access.........................
You also need to consider if children, especially if young, will understand your questions (etc) and whether, if the subject is a sensitive one, you may upset/damage children in any way. There is also the question of demand characteristics, children because they are immature may react dishonestly – to give the researcher what they want, or to impress their peer group.'

Practice doing this for different methods.
e.g. *Questionnaires have a number of advantages when researching education. Because they are usually anonymous children (or teachers) may fill them in honestly, especially if the topic is a sensitive one, and it may be easier to get consent - from heads, teachers, parents etc because they are less intrusive than interviews etc. But younger children may not understand the questions..................................*
Finish the paragraph, using the general advantages disadvantages of questionnaires but applying them to children/teachers, parents etc

Level 3 marks
To get level 3 marks – up to 20 you need to make **3 or more well explained points connecting the method to the actual topic.**

This involves **application** – you can't be taught every possible connection between every topic and method – you have to 'think on your feet'. You can however practice and prepare.

If, for example, we were doing an essay on the topic of (e.g) *the effects of school processes (labelling, teachers attitudes, hidden curriculum' on pupils educational performance) using (e.g.) unstructured interviews?* The following would be examples of the different levels of analysis:

(Question 1) *'Using unstructured interviews would be one of the best ways of studying the effects of streaming on educational performance, because students would be able to explain, in their own words, whether they had suffered from labelling.'* **(Level 1 - just method).**

'Moreover because to study streaming you may need to interview young children, who are intellectually immature, they may not understand some of the concepts and words in a questionnaire whereas you can explain questions to them in an interview and allow them to respond in their own words, thus making the results more valid (true to life)'. (Level 2 – social characteristics of children)
'Streaming can be a very damaging process so you would need to be sensitive in your approach towards pupils who may have suffered from being put into low streams and so not trust authority

figures like teachers or researchers. With unstructured interviews you can build up a rapport with children so that they trust you. They are then more likely to open up and give the researcher in depth, valid answers about how they have been effected by streaming, for example loss of confidence or alienation from school.' (Level 3 – topic and method)

Practice looking at different methods and topics and practice this skill of application.

Here are some examples to help you practice:

1.Applying material (from the item) and your knowledge of research methods, evaluate the strengths and limitations of using postal questionnaires to study differences in educational attainment amongst different social classes.
2. Applying material (from the item) and your knowledge of research methods, evaluate the strengths and limitations of using and weaknesses of using participant observation to study bullying in schools..

3. Applying material (from the item) and your knowledge of research methods, evaluate the strengths and limitations of using of using personal documents (diaries, letters,essays etc) to study racial prejudice and discrimination in schools.

Think of your own examples

Another crucial tip when answering Q5 is to **use the item** – in the item there will be two or three points about the topic/method you can **develop** (not just copy out!). The item is there to help you – use it.

<u>**Note – You do not have to use studies in this question – even to get full marks, in fact be careful about using studies, they must be applied not just described.**</u>

The Exam
Preparation and Revision

Revision should starts on the first day of your AS course. Just reading through the work you do each day is an excellent way of re-inforcing your knowledge and understanding. Unfortunately few of us have the discipline to do this! What most of us can do, however is to make sure we attend well, do all the assignments we are set and revise for the tests and exams that come along during the course.

Revision is not about cramming in the few weeks (or even days before) the exam. The students who do best in exams are generally those who work consistently throughout the year.

Revision, in the period before the exam, is about **reinforcing and overlearning** the material you have been learning throughout your course, and **practicing the essential skill**s that you will need to answer the questions on the paper.

What's the best way of doing this?

Writers have made a lot of money out of revision books. Sometimes the advice they give you on how to revise seems to take longer to process that the stuff you actually need to learn! People are, of course, individuals and successful revision can take a number of different forms. However there are a few 'golden rules' that can help you:

Starting revision

Bear in mind that revision is not something you just do at the end of the course, it is a continuous process. However for you're final revision I would suggest stating in the Easter holidays – most of your course should be finished by them and you will have a lot of free time.

The dreaded Revision Timetable!

Some of the 'helpful' guides to making a revision timetable that I have seen are so complicated and time consuming that, if you followed them to the letter, you'd be left with very little time to revise! The best revision timetables involve simply dividing (all your subjects) into topics, filling them into a calendar or diary and making sure you stick to it!

Basic Revision Techniques

First of all, of course, you have to learn the stuff. Try this basic technique. Read through a topic/subtopic two or three times, highlight any key theory, concepts and studies etc.. Take a piece of paper and wite down all you can remember. Then go back to the notes and see what you have missed. Add these to the notes you have just made, **in a different colour ink**. Read these though again concentrating on the stuff you had not remembered (people spend a lot of tiime revising things they already know). Then go on to your next topic.

Variations

1. Try making **brain-maps** of a topic instead of writing notes. Psychologists tell us we should use three colours in brain-maps so, if you trust psychologists, try that! Again add stuff you haven't remembered in a different colour.

2. Make big, **colourful posters** of different topics and stick them on your bedroom wall, then you can't miss them!

3. Draw **diagrams and pictures,** if you are the visual or artistic type, to help you remember.

4. Make **summaries of topics** and put them onto **small revision cards** that you can easily carry around with you, so you can revise on the bus or train etc.

5. **Record your notes** and listen to them on your Ipod, mobile phone etc. Again you can do this anywhere, even walking along the street. Think of how you learn songs without even trying, just by continuous listening. Maybe you could even sing them into your recording device – 'Sociology Rap 1' – Family Diversity! (Or maybe not!).

The point is that you can use a lot of different techniques to give you variety and make 'learning stuff' a bit less boring. (I've read books that claim reising can be fun, like you I don't believe them!).

And remember, very few, if any of us can remember everything. The point is to remember enough to be able to apply your knowledge and understanding to answer exam questions. **It is not simply a question of what you know, it is how you use that knowledge.**

Triggers

Your aim should be to reduce your revision notes to the bear minimum, so that a single word or phrase will trigger, in your mind, a whole lot of material that you have learned. Let's take an example:

Say you were revising Marxist theory in Education. Your triggers which you reduce your notes to might be:

<u>Key concepts/theory/studies</u>
Material deprivation – (Boudon)
Cultural Reproduction – Cultural Capital and Cultural Deficit (Bourdieu)
Correspondence theory – (Bowles and Gintis)
I.S.A. -, Ruling Class ideology, legitimation, hegemony,
Willis 'the Lads' etc..............................

<u>Evaluation</u>
Deterministic
Social mobility etc

These basic studies and concepts should trigger off in your mind the detailed knowledge and understanding that relates to each concept/theory/study.

Over-learning/Reinforcement

This is simple. You need to reinforce your knowledge/learning by going over material again at a later date. A simple technique. Before you start your new revision topics for the day read through what you learned yesterday. Re-read it again a week later. Build this in to your revision timetable.

Theory

Make theory the most important part of your revision. Not only are there specific questions (especially essays) on theory, but theory will help you answer any essay question. Indeed you cannot attain the highest marks without theory. Take the family for example. If you have an essay question on divorce, single parent families, family diversity etc. etc. an excellent way to approach it would be to use Functionalism, Feminism, the New Right, and what they have to say on the issue. This will also help you to evaluate, by comparing and contrasting the theories. The same apllies to Education and Methods questions.

Skills and Practice

Revision is not just about learning stuff, it is about practicing the skills you will need to do well in your exams. You will, of course, have been doing this throughout the year, but as you are coming up for the actual exams it becomes increasingly important. I have marked many papers where the student obviously knows a lot, but fails to apply it to the question they have been asked.

Exam Papers

Get hold of as many **exam papers** as you can (there easily available from AQA over the net – and free to print off) and go through the questions, **interpreting them** and **practicing answers**. A good technique is to do this with a friend (a point that applies to all revision, as long as you don't spend your time talking about what you did last night and discussing the latest Beyonce CD!). You should spend at least as much time writing when you revise as you do reading.

Make sure **you are familiar with the skills you need** – Knowledge and understanding, interpretation and application, and especially analysis and evaluation as these are the skills you will need to get high marks.

Do extra exam questions – there are lots in this book, and ask your teacher to look at your answers, most sociology teachers are very kind and will only be too pleased to help!

Main References and Sources
P. Aries, Centuries of Childhood, Penguin, 1962
M. Arnot, M.E. David and G. Weiner, Closing the Gender Gap: Post-war Education and Social Change, Polity Press; Blackwell, 1999
0. Banks, The Sociology of Education, Batsford, 1971
E. Barker, The Making of a Moonie: Brainwashing or Choice? Blackwell, 1984
H.S. Becker, 'Social-class Variations in the Teacher-Pupil Relationship', in B. Cosin (ed.), School and Society: A Sociological Reader, Routledge & Kegan Paul, 1971
B. Bernstein, 'Social Class and Linguistic Development: A Theory of Social Learning', in A.H. Halsey, J. Floud and C.A. Anderson (eds.), Education, Economy and Society, Free Press, 1961
B.B. Bernstein, Class, Codes and Control, Routh Kegan Paul, 1971
E. Bott, Family and Social Network, Tavistock, 1 M.G. Boulton, On Being a Mother, Tavistock, 1'
P. Bourdieu and J. C. Passeron, 'Cultural Reproduction and Social Reproduction', in R.K. Brown (ed.), Knowledge, Education and Cultural Change, Tavistok Press 1973
P. Bourdieu and J. C. Passerson, Reproduction in Education, Society and Culture, Sage, 1977
P. Bourgois, In Search of Respect – Selling Crack in El Barrio – Cambridge University Press Second Edition, 2003

S. Bowles and H. Gintis, Schooling in Capitalist Educational Reform and the Contradictions of Economic Life, Routledge & Kegan Paul, 1976

R. Chester, 'The Rise of the Neo-conventioni New Society, 9 May 1985

A.V. Cicourel, The Social Organization of Juvenile justice, Heinemann, 1976

M. Cole, Bowles and Gintis Revisited: Correspondence and Contradiction in Educational Theory, Palmer Press, 1988

D. Cooper, The Death of the Family, Penguin, 1972

K. Davis and W Moore, 'Some Principles of stratification', in R. Bendix and S. Lipset (eds), Class, tatus and Power 2nd edn), Routledge & Kegan Paul,
1967

R. Dobash and R. Dobash, Violence against Wives, Open looks, 1980

G. Driver and R. Ballard, 'Comparing Performance in a multi-racial School: South Asian Pupils at 16-plus', New Thmmunity, VII, 143-53, 1979

E. Durkheim, The Division of Labour in Society, The Free Press 1947

S. Edgell. Middle class families, Allen and Unwin 1980

F. Engels. The Origin of the Family, private Property and the State, Lawrence and Wishart, 1972

E. Ferri and K. Smith, Parenting in the 1990s,Family Policy Studies Centre. 1996

M. Fuller, 'Black Girls in a Comprehensive School', in M. Hammersley and P. Woods (eds), Life in School: The Sociology of Pupil Culture, Open University Press, 1982

J. Gershunny, 'The Domestic Labour Revolution', in M. Anderson, F. Bechhofer and J. Gershunny (eds) The Social and Political Economy of the Household, Oxford University Press, 1994

J. Gershunny and H. Laurie, 'Couples, Work and Money', in R. Berthoud and J. Gershunny (eds(Seven Years in the Lives of British Families, Policy Press, 2000

S. Gewirtz, S. Ball and R. Bowe, Markets, Choice, and Equity in Education, Open University Press, 1995

J.G. Ghevarughese, 'Foundations of Eurocentrism in Mathematics', Race and Class, 28(13), 1987

A. Giddens, Sociology (5th edn), Polity Press, 2001

D. Gillborn, 'Race', Ethnicity and Education: Teaching and Learning in Multi-ethnic Schools, Unwin Hyman, 1990

D. Gillborn and D. Youdell, Rationing Education: Policy, Practice, Reform, and Equity, Open University Press, 2000

E. Goffman, The Presentation of Self in Everyday Life, University of Edinburgh Social Sciences Research Centre, 1959

F. Goffman, Asylums: Essays on the Social Situation of Mental Patients and Other Inmates, Penguin, 1968

R. Gomm, Social Research Methodology: A Critical Introduction, Palgrave Macmillan, 2004

D. Hargreaves, Social Relations in a Secondary School, Routledge & Kegan, 1973

D.H. Hargreaves, S. Hester and F.J. Mellor, Deviance in Classrooms, Routledge & Kegan Paul, 1975

L. Harker, Chance of a Lifetime: The Impact of Bad Housing on Children's Lives, 2006, from http://england.shelter.org.uk/files/seealsodocs/23199/ Lifechancereport%2Epdf

B. Jackson and D. Marsden, Education and the Class, Routledge, 1962

R. Jowell (ed.), The British Social Attitudes Surv Ashgate, 1984, 1991, 1997

Man-Yee Kan, 'Gender Asymmetry in the Division of Domestic Labour', paper presented to the British Household Panel Survey, Institute for Social and Economic Research, 6 July 2001

N.G. Keddie, Tinker, Tailor: The Myth of Cultural Deprivation, Penguin Education, 1973

A. Kelly, Final Report of the GIST Project, Science for Girls, Open University 1987

R.D. Laing and A. Esterson, Sanity, Madness an Family, Penguin, 1964

M. Mac an Ghaill, Young, Gifted and Black Student Teacher Relations in the Schooling of Black Youth, University Press, 1988

M. Mac an Ghaill, The Making of Men: Masculine Sexualities and Schooling, Open University Press

P. McNeil and S. Chapman, Research Methods, Routledge, 2005

I. Mirza, Young, Female and Black, Routledge, 1992

L. Morris, The Workings of the Household, Polity, 1990 G.P. Murdock, Social Structure, Macmillan, 1949

C. Murray, The Emerging British Underclass, Institute for Economic Affairs, 1990

C. Murray, Underclass: The Crisis Deepens, Institute for Economic Affairs, 1994

A. Oakley, Sex Gender and Society, Temple Smith, 1972

A. Oakley. Housewife, Allen lane, 1974

A. Oakley, The Sociology of Housework, Martin Robertson 1974

Office for National Statistics

J. Pahl, Money and Marriage, Macmillan, 1989

T. Parsons, The Social System, Free Press, 1951

T. Parsons, 'The Social Structure of the Family', in R.N. Anshen (ed.), The Family: Its Functions and Destiny, Harper & Row, 1959

T. Parsons, 'The School Class as a Social System', in A.H. Halsey, J. Floud and C.A. Anderson, Education, Economy and Society, The Free Press, 1961

J. Patrick, A Glasgow Gang Observed, Eyre Methuen, 1973

M. Phillips, The Sex-change Society: Feminised Britain and the Neutered Male, Social Market Foundation, 1999

N. Postman, The Disappearance of Childhood, Vintage, 1994

R. Rapoport and R. Rapoport, Families in Britain, Routledge & Kegan , 1982

D. Rosenhan, 'On Being Sane in Insane Places', Science,
179, 250-8, 1973

R. Rosenthal and L. Jacobson, Pygmalion in the Classroom: Teacher Expectation and Pupil's Intellectual Development, Crown House, 2003

T Sewell, Black Masculinities and Schooling. How Black Boys Survive Modern Schooling, Trentham, 1997

S. Sharpe, Just Like a Girl: How Girls Learn to be Women, Penguin 1976, 1994

D. Spender, Invisible Women, Woman's Press, 1983

M. Stanworth, Gender and Schooling: A Study of Sexual Division in the Classroom, Hutchinson, 1983

B. Sugarman, Social Class, Values and Behaviour, Penguin, 1970

P. Townsend, D. Gordon, S. Nandy, C. Pantazis and S.
Pemberton, 'Child Poverty in the Developing World', Townsend Centre for International Poverty Research, Policy Press, 2003

K. Trobe, Revising AS Sociological Methods, Lindisfarne Press, 2001

W. Whyte, Street Corner Society, University of Chicago Press, 1955

P. Willis, Learning to Labour: How Working-class Kids Get Working-class Jobs, Saxon House, 1977

C. Wright, 'Black Students—White Teachers', in B. Troyna (ed.), Racial Inequality in Education, Tavistock, 1987

M. Young and P. Willmott, The Sytmmetrical Family, Penguin, 1973